GW00659362

THE NEW MOTORCYCLE YEARBOOK

3

NCR
31

THE NEW MOTORCYCLE YEARBOOK

3

The Definitive Annual Guide to All New Motorcycles Worldwide

Simon de Burton

MERRELL
LONDON • NEW YORK

YAMAHA

MERRELL
First Published 2007 by
Merrell Publishers Limited

Head office
81 Southwark Street
London SE1 0HX

New York office
740 Broadway, 12th Floor
New York, NY 10003

merrellpublishers.com

British Library Cataloguing-in-Publication Data:
De Burton, Simon
The new motorcycle yearbook 3 : the definitive annual guide to all new motorcycles worldwide
1. Motorcycles – Periodicals 2. Motorcycles – Design and construction – Periodicals
I. Title
629.2'275'05

ISBN-13: 978-1-8589-4379-4
ISBN-10: 1-8589-4379-5

Produced by Merrell Publishers Limited
Designed by Untitled
Copy-edited by Richard Dawes
Proof-read by Elizabeth Tatham

Printed and bound in Singapore

Page 2
NCR New Blue, see pp. 186–87
Pages 4–5
Yamaha Giggle, see pp. 210–11
Pages 8–9
Confederate Hellcat 20Ltd, see pp. 138–39
Pages 20–21
Yamaha YZF-R1, see pp. 46–47
Pages 48–49
Aprilia RXV 450i, see pp. 52–53
Pages 70–71
Yamaha XVS1300A Midnight Star, see pp. 92–93
Pages 94–95
Moto Morini MM3, see pp. 110–111
Pages 114–15
Moto Guzzi Norge 850, see pp. 120–21
Pages 126–27
Suzuki GSF 1250SA Bandit, see pp. 170–71
Pages 176–77
NCR New Blue, see pp. 186–87
Pages 190–91
Yamaha X-Max 250, see pp. 212–13
Pages 214–15
Can-Am Spyder, see pp. 216–17
Pages 252–53
Suzuki GSX-R1000, see pp. 42–43
Pages 268–69
Kawasaki Versys, see pp. 152–53
Page 270
Harley-Davidson XR1200, see pp. 144–45

For Cosmo Francis de Burton,
born 24 January 2007

CONTENTS

Forcewinder

TRENDS, HIGHLIGHTS AND PREDICTIONS

It is some twenty years since the development of road-going production motorcycles entered the revolutionary era of the middleweight, race-replica sports bike with the launch, during the late 1980s, of such machines as the Honda CBR600 and the Yamaha FZR600. Until then a 'middleweight' invariably had to be a 550-cc, four-cylinder 'all-rounder' with an upright riding position, no fairing, an exposed, air-cooled engine and comfortable seating for two. These were transitional machines bought by riders who were gradually making their way up from the 250-cc bikes on which they had learned to ride to the 750-cc or one-litre road-burners of their dreams. Handling of the 550-fours was just about adequate and performance was reasonable, given the fact that many of them were not much lighter than their larger-engined brothers.

The introduction by Honda and Yamaha of the then odd-sounding '600' class caused an almost immediate reversal of the situation. Suddenly the most exciting motorcycles you could buy were such middleweights as the CBR and the FZ because their high-tech, water-cooled engines were tuned to produce at least as much power as their 750-cc contemporaries, yet they were fitted into scaled-down, lightweight frames complemented by stiff suspension, aerodynamic sports fairings and race-style riding positions.

This whole package produced a type of motorcycle that, until it arrived, had seemed an impossible dream. But now here was a supersports machine that was a thrill to ride and had a screaming engine and pin-sharp handling, yet was sufficiently docile and usable at low revs to provide practical everyday transport. Suzuki and Kawasaki quickly followed the lead of Honda and Yamaha, and for the past two decades the 'big four' have made an annual ritual of leapfrogging one another to produce a faster, lighter, more powerful and better-handling supersports 600 than the previous title holder.

Of course, the manufacturers would not have been doing so had it not been for the seemingly insatiable appetite of the buying public for machines of this type: bikes that look and perform as though they belong on the racetrack but in truth spend most of their lives commuting through a tangle of city traffic.

Change appears to be afoot, however. *The New Motorcycle Yearbook 2* announced the arrival of the latest, truly stunning 600s from Suzuki, Triumph and Yamaha. This year we complete the line-up with details of the new Honda CBR600RR (pp. 32–33) and Kawasaki's Ninja ZX-6R (pp. 34–35), but other than these there are no truly new sports middleweights to talk about.

The fact is, supersports 600s appear to have gone a bit too far. While no red-blooded motorcyclist could resist falling in love with a machine such as the current Yamaha YZF-R1, most would have to admit that its dinky dimensions and full race-riding position make it rather impractical for a trip to the shops. Anyway, do we really need 98 kW (131 bhp) at 14,500 rpm and a top speed of 265 km/h (165 mph) simply to get to work on time? With small fuel tanks giving poor long-distance capability,

In keeping with the growing demand, manufacturers are seeking to tempt us with ever more interesting, cool-looking and comfortable yet hot-performing street bikes.

The typical Japanese middleweights of the 1970s, such as the Honda CB550 Four (bottom left) were a far cry from the aerodynamic, light and powerful sports 600s that followed; pictured are Yamaha's Thundercat (top left) and Honda's CBR600F (above).

engines that produce little low-end torque, and high-mounted footpegs that demand a jockey crouch, the latest generation of uncompromising 'racetrack refugees' has led many riders to decide that sacrificing comfort and practicality in order to look like a GP star on the way to the office is perhaps not really worthwhile.

As a result, middleweights that fill the gap left by the rather stodgy 550-fours of the 1980s are rapidly stealing sales from their supersports cousins and, in keeping with the growing demand, manufacturers are seeking to tempt us with ever more interesting, cool-looking and comfortable yet hot-performing street bikes that have upright riding positions and a decent fuel range.

It will come as no surprise, then, that this edition's Street, Naked and Muscle section (pp. 126–75) contains several new models powered by mid-sized engines, such as the Yamaha FZ6, the Kawasaki Versys, Honda's market-leading Hornet and, with a 750-cc engine, Kawasaki's newest and most covetable take on the Z750.

The popularity of supermoto and trail-style machines also continues to grow, with new versions from BMW, KTM and Aprilia (see pp. 48–69), while the Adventure Sports trend, which really took off about three years ago, looks set to attract even more riders to such purposeful, long-distance bikes as the Benelli Amazonas and Triumph's all-new 1050-cc Tiger (see pp. 94–113).

However, that doesn't mean the end of the road for supersports bikes; far from it: the one-litre-plus group is boosted by such ultra-desirable offerings as Ducati's 1098 (just what the firm needed to counteract ailing sales of the 'old' 999), MV Agusta's super-expensive F4 1100 and the class-leading Suzuki GSX-R1000. This category, too, appears to be attracting motorcyclists with both money and a desire to own something different. For them this year brings such rolling works of art as the Bimota Tesi 3D, the NCR Millona track-only bike and the Ducati 999-based Steffano Café9 (see pp. 20–47).

Yet it is in the formerly less innovative categories that some of the most interesting technical developments in motorcycling appear to be taking place. In the Oddball section (pp. 214–37) you can read about the fully enclosed, torpedo-like Monotracer and four machines that introduce a third wheel to motorcycling: the Can-Am Spyder, the Gilera Fuoco, the Piaggio MP3 and the electrically powered Vectrix 3W.

The last three of these are intended to instil confidence in inexperienced riders and those who have always been put off powered two-wheelers by the belief that they are unstable. (Judging by a recent survey carried out by an insurance organization, which showed that the most crashed machines in the United Kingdom are Vespa ET4s ridden in London, they may be right.)

The Fuoco, MP3 and Vectrix 3W corner like a conventional scooter, but their additional front wheels ensure that they cannot 'fall over' at low speeds. Other novelties to lure new riders include the seven-speed, electrically operated gearbox that is fitted to Honda's new Forza Smart 2-Seater (pp. 198–99). This unusual machine also comes with a demountable AVN

Be it an electrically powered Vectrix 3W three-wheeler (above, left), a petrol-engined Piaggio MP3 (top), or a supermoto-styled Husqvarna STR (above), motorcycles in all their forms offer a practical urban transport solution.

(audiovisual navigation) system, which not only plays music but also tells the rider how to get to his or her intended destination and allows communication with a passenger via a wireless intercom that is part of an entertainment system .

Another 'bright' idea that we could see on bikes in the not-too-distant future is bodywork made from light-emitting panels that show up in low visibility. And the design genius Massimo Tamburini, creator of the iconic Ducati 916, has come up with a supermoto machine for Husqvarna that has adjustable frame geometry to make it suitable for either commuting or extreme competition (see pp. 62–63).

So, with plenty of fabulous motorcycles to choose from and many brilliant ideas either coming to fruition or waiting in the wings, the future of motorcycling must be assured. Or is it?

Even though a powered two-wheeler is undoubtedly one of the most efficient ways of simultaneously beating urban gridlock, providing an 'independent transport solution', combating pollution and, of course, having some fun, there still appears to be a faction at work in most countries that wants motorcycles sidelined.

As someone who has been riding a motorcycle in and around London for twenty-five years, I've seen a lot of bureaucratic poppycock come and go. The latest piece to rattle my cage is the proposed (and certain to happen) introduction of metered motorcycle parking bays in the capital. The governing body that thought up this idea has, remarkably, tried to blame the urgency for introducing the scheme on the fact that car drivers have been exploiting a loophole in the regulations that allows them to park in motorcycle bays without risking a fine. This would seem almost plausible were it not for the fact that it hardly ever happens. I think that I have witnessed such inconsiderate parking not even a handful of times in all the years I have been a motorcyclist.

The real reasons behind the scheme are that many people – hard-done-by motorists in particular – don't like the fact that motorcyclists can currently park for free, and, more significantly, the local authorities hate to think that they are missing out on a revenue stream that might help make up a shortfall in the cash given to them by central government.

In a shameless act of cynicism, officials have said that motorcycle parking meters are being introduced to make life much better for all of us. In reality it simply means that the already inadequate provision of space will be further reduced as each parking bay will take a set number of machines and no more. At present,at least there is the chance of finding a space, however small it may be and frustrating to get into and out of, between the tightly packed rows of freely parked machines.

What the authorities should be doing is assessing the suitability of the swathes of free road space in London and other cities around the world that are presently designated as no-parking zones for cars. In many cases these areas would easily and safely accommodate up to twenty motorcycles. Or we could follow the French and

Motorcycles are ideal for negotiating city traffic, but as more people use them so must adequate parking be provided.

let motorcyclists park almost anywhere that there is a free space where a stationary motorcycle does not interfere with pedestrian or vehicular traffic. Allowing riders to exercise consideration and common sense in this way seems to work perfectly well in Paris, so why shouldn't it be the same anywhere else?

Another totally predictable discovery is the one announced in a report commissioned by Transport for London (TFL) that has, conveniently for the fine-mongers, decided that motorcycles and bus lanes don't mix. It is hardly rocket science to deduce that motorcycles and scooters will almost always flow freely along a lane that contains no cars other than taxis; nor is it difficult to believe that any biker will be safer with fewer cars in the immediate vicinity. So it would seem to be an excellent idea to allow motorbikes to use bus lanes. Well, not according to the TFL report, which concludes that the idea is 'not supported'. Strangely, no one asked me if I support it; nor did they ask any of the dozens of motorcyclists that I know.

The fact is, motorcyclists are a somewhat practically minded bunch who can usually find a way around a problem, so it wouldn't surprise me if, for example, it became the norm for riders to travel with two sets of number plates: the correct set for road riding and a handy, Velcro-backed interchangeable second set with an 'inadvertently' misplaced digit, to be used for parking purposes only. This practice would certainly reduce the number of unnecessary tickets brought about by the latest parking 'improvements'.

However, laws that turn honest, decent people into reluctant criminals are not good laws in the first place, and the last thing we want is for motorcyclists to be returned to 'rebel' status, even if we would be rebels most definitely *with* a cause.

Fortunately, the many pro-motorcycling lobby groups across the world, from the United States to Australia and everywhere in between, are working tirelessly against needless legislation and misguided anti-bike thinking to promote and protect motorcycling as we now know it. Ultimately, however, we are the people who are really going to save the day: riders and enthusiasts who are willing to take a stand when the bureaucrats go a step too far.

HONDA'S MOTORCYCLE REVOLUTION

To many European-based motorcycle enthusiasts, November is an important month. In the United Kingdom, while it usually marks the start of a long winter of biking discontent that can make our favourite form of transport seem decidedly less attractive than it does during the long, occasionally hot, days of summer, it is also the month when the following year's machines are revealed to the public for the first time, at such glitzy events as Milan's EICMA and the UK's International Motorcycle and Scooter Show.

November 2006 was important for another reason, too, because it marked the centenary of the birth of perhaps the most influential figure in the history of motorcycling aside from Gottlieb Daimler (who invented the petrol-powered two-wheeler in 1885). By now you may have guessed that I am referring to none other than Soichiro Honda, founder of the eponymous engineering company that is now recognized in every corner of the world, no matter how small, for producing everything from generators to cars and from powerboats to lawnmowers – and, of course, motorcycles.

Soichiro Honda was born on 17 November 1906, the son of a blacksmith and weaver. From an early age he was so interested in machinery that whenever he saw a mechanical object he felt obliged to dismantle it to try to discover how it worked. In later life he recalled the first time he saw a car passing through the Japanese village in which he was raised and chased after it on foot for almost 1 km (0.6 mile), determined to overcome his bafflement as to how it was moving under its own power.

Like many highly successful people, Honda had a burning desire to learn yet almost no formal education. Fortunately, his father's transition from blacksmith and weaver to bicycle repairer appears to have led Honda junior to his vocation more successfully than any number of examination certificates because it spurred him on to seek work as a garage apprentice. At the age of twenty-two he started his own motor-repair business and, always passionate about racing, even built his own racing car using an adapted V8 engine taken from a scrap aircraft.

But it was the austerity of the post-war years that brought about a turning point in Honda's career and indeed in the motorcycle industry in general. Responding to the need for an inexpensive form of transport that would carry workers both further and faster than the traditional bicycle, Honda began to design a powered two-wheeler that he called the A-Type.

This machine was as rudimentary as motorcycles come and, although it functioned and promised cheap mobility, it was not up to the standards that the exacting Honda had anticipated. His next attempt, however, was. The 98-cc, two-stroke D-Type of 1947 was essentially a sturdy bicycle with an engine mounted between the frame tubes that drove the rear wheel via a belt. Rather than the short 'tin-can' silencers used on similar engines, such as the British-built Cyclemaster, the D-Type had a recognizable exhaust system and, most importantly of all, a crossbar-mounted fuel tank emblazoned with the magic word 'Honda'.

Responding to the need for an inexpensive form of transport ... Honda began to design a powered two-wheeler that he called the A-Type.

The ability to innovate has been one of Honda's key strengths throughout its history. Benchmark designs have ranged from the post-war D-Type (top left) to the 750-Four of the late 1960s (bottom left), and on to today's state-of-the-art, four-stroke dirt bikes (above).

Back then, Honda was just another small, insignificant producer of lightweight, powered two-wheelers, and no different from hundreds of manufacturers in Europe and the USA – and certainly of no relevance to established producers of such 'real' motorcycles as Norton, Triumph and Harley-Davidson. So it was no surprise that few took notice when Honda said that his firm would compete in the Isle of Man TT races little more than a decade after he had developed his first commercially viable machine.

Honda made its debut at the Isle of Man in 1959, leaving as an 'also ran', yet in 1961 Mike Hailwood won the ultra-lightweight and lightweight TTs on Honda machines, and soon the factory race bikes – engineered to a hitherto unseen standard – were wiping the floor with the opposition, with such multiple victories as that achieved by Jim Redman in 1964, when he became the only motorcycle racer to win three GP races on the same day by taking the chequered flag in the 125-cc, 250-cc and 350-cc classes at Assen: all, of course, on Hondas.

Such performances were exactly what Honda had hoped for, as they demonstrated just how exceptional the company's machines were and brought them to the attention of the mass market that they were aiming to seize. As longer-established marques fell by the wayside, Honda went from strength to strength, finally sounding the death knell for the old-style British motorcycle industry in 1969 with the launch of the CB750 Four, the machine regarded as the world's first 'superbike'.

And, as Honda had been growing its business, so the other 'big three' Japanese motorcycle producers had been establishing themselves: Kawasaki since 1949, Yamaha from the mid-1950s, and Suzuki, which was founded in 1936 but only started to become a significant force, like Honda, during the early 1960s.

In the years between Soichiro Honda's birth and the time that he laid down the roots of his business, more than 150 small motorcycle manufacturers operating around the world, mainly in the United Kingdom, France, Germany and the United States, had either come and gone or had continued trying to establish themselves by making essentially hand-built machines in small numbers, mostly for a home market.

What Honda demonstrated, however, was that this was not the way forward: hand-built motorcycles with too much variation in quality, reliability and performance from one machine to another were not the way to establish one's worldwide reputation. This could be done only by offering proven products built to the same standard and ideally sold at an affordable price, just as Henry Ford had discovered with the Model T.

Honda's most successful realization of this strategy was undoubtedly the Super Cub, which was launched in 1958 and in 2006 became the first motor vehicle to reach a production figure of a staggering 50 million units. The twenty-first-century Super Cub, also known as the C100, remains almost identical in appearance to the original and continues to fulfil Soichiro Honda's dream of providing affordable transport for the masses.

Sadly for dozens of less efficient, less marketing-savvy manufacturers, the invasion of powered two-wheelers

from Japan proved too much to compete with, and by the 1980s, when the motorcycle market was in the doldrums throughout the world, most buyers of new machines chose a bike made by one of the 'big four', leaving only a tiny share of the market to more exotic manufacturers such as Ducati, Moto Guzzi and Harley-Davidson. In those days even sales of BMW bikes, now growing healthily, were pathetically low.

During the past decade (and especially, by happy coincidence, since the first edition of *The New Motorcycle Yearbook* appeared in 2005), however, the tide has started to turn and, while the giant manufacturers continue to make superlative machines at all levels, demand has returned for products built by smaller brands, often bearing legendary names from the past.

Triumph is back with a vengeance; Ducati is regaining the popularity it enjoyed before a few questionable design decisions alienated it from some of its fans; and such names as Benelli, CCM, Derbi, KTM, Moto Guzzi, Moto Morini and Victory are offering something different to motorcyclists who like to stand out from the crowd.

So, against all the odds, the industry is to some extent returning to the days of old, when many small makers offered a huge choice of models. This has come about for a variety of reasons, one of which is that motorcycles are increasingly regarded as 'luxury goods'. Many models are something to have in the garage for when the fancy takes you, rather like a yacht or a classic car; not so much an object for practical use but something with which to express one's individuality, success and wealth. Why else would MV Agusta, for example, have produced the £67,000 F4 1100, and why else would order lists for Ducati's £40,000 Desmosedici road-going racer stretch into late 2008?

Fortunately for motorcycling, for so long regarded by the bigoted and uninitiated as an activity to be enjoyed only by the lower echelons of society, people with style and influence have made riding a bike rather a chic thing to do. At the same time, the luxury-goods industry as a whole has been democratized by a massive increase in wealth around the world that has allowed more people to discover new things with the help of their equally newly acquired cash.

Interestingly, however, the very thing that once made luxury goods 'luxurious' has now been superseded, and this is that they had to be handmade from scratch. Be it motorcycles or wristwatches, luggage or motor cars, luxury used to mean a craftsman working away for hours, days, weeks, or even months to produce one or two examples of a supremely well-made object that could be sold for enough money to justify his time and give him a decent profit.

Nowadays, with the availability of computer-aided machine tools and high-tech design software, it would be absurd for a watchmaker to file every tooth of a gear wheel by hand, just as it would be both pointless and inefficient for a builder of motorcycles to cut every piece of metal for his machine with tin snips. The fact is, parts can now be made faster and to a far higher

Left
Honda showed the rest of the world how to mass-produce successfully machines of high quality.
Above
Rare limited editions have taken motorcycles into the league of luxury goods. Pictured here are MV Agusta's F4 1100 (top) and Ducati's Desmosedici (centre and bottom).

Demand from buyers for different-looking machines has led to a growth in the number of small firms offering limited-production models or hand-built conversions based on such popular motorcycles as Triumph's bestselling Bonneville.

standard than they ever could be in the old days, and computerized machinery is accurate to a degree impossible for a person to achieve, which means quite simply that more 'luxury' goods can be made in less time and with a better finish than ever before.

Add the fact that many famous names (in motorcycles and in other fields) are now owned by conglomerates with huge marketing budgets and worldwide penetration, and the reason for the return of the ostensibly 'niche' manufacturer becomes clear. There is a place for MV Agusta, Moto Morini, Buell, Triumph and others because so many of us like to appear 'different' – that is, not buyers of the Universal Japanese Motorcycle – and we don't want a Honda, Suzuki, Kawasaki or Yamaha. Instead, what we want is a motorcycle that starts when we want it to, does not break down, goes, stops and handles as well as a Japanese one, and is made just as well, if not better.

What has happened over the century since Soichiro Honda's birth is that the motorcycle business has come full circle, evolving from an industry driven by numerous, small-scale manufacturers to one dominated by a handful of major players and now into one in which those major players can live side by side with the 'little guys' that offer something different for those to whom motorcycling means more than just a means of getting to work or beating city traffic.

My prediction is that during the next decade this trend will not only continue but will gather momentum, as large companies (which, quite possibly, have nothing to do with motorcycle manufacture at present) latch on to the fact that bikes provide fun and freedom in a far more accessible, more easily enjoyed way than, for example, supercars or powerboats, and that the trend offers hitherto unrealized potential for selling beautifully built, high-level machines to select buyers at correspondingly handsome prices.

For the foreseeable future there will, of course, remain a market for Honda's ubiquitous Super Cub and for every road-burner, commuter bike and dual-purpose machine that Japan can produce, but there will be a lot more available from other, smaller manufacturers at the high end, which means greater awareness of our favourite subject among people with influence. And that can only be good for motorcycling as a whole.

THE MOTORCYCLES

SPORTS

YAMAHA
YAMAHA

BENELLI TORNADO 1130

Engine
1130 cc, double-overhead-camshaft, three-cylinder, four-stroke
Power
92 kW (123 bhp) @ 9000 rpm
Torque
114 Nm (84 ft lb) @ 6250 rpm
Gearbox
Six-speed
Final drive
Chain
Weight
185 kg (408 lb)
Top speed
241 km/h (150 mph)

Benelli is one of the oldest and greatest of Italian motorcycle marques. Founded in 1911, it enjoyed success on road and track for decades, but a general downturn in motorcycle sales in the 1980s saw it decline into a maker of nothing more exciting than a range of scooters and mopeds. Production of 'real' motorcycles resumed in 1999, however, after the company was purchased by a major investor, and Benelli's rebirth was celebrated with the launch of the stunning-looking Tornado.

In addition to its beautiful lines and rear-mounted radiator – complete with underseat cooling fans – the Tornado was also notable for its huge price tag: at around £13,000 in the United Kingdom, it was almost double the cost of some of its Japanese counterparts. That, combined with problems of reliability, led to slow sales, and demand for the original, 900-cc Tornado soon fizzled out.

Now under Chinese ownership, the brand continues to produce some great machines, such as the recent Tre-K, the TNT and the all-new Amazonas adventure sports bike (see pp. 96–97). The new Tornado retains those gorgeous looks but benefits from being more affordable and, most importantly, being fitted with the latest 1130-cc engine used in the rest of the range. More reliable and more powerful than the troublesome 900-cc unit, this should give the Tornado the second chance that it deserves.

Benelli

Benelli

BIMOTA TESI 3D

Bimota motorcycles used to be about the most exotic two-wheelers you could buy. They were built in tiny numbers, cost a relative fortune and were a rare sight on the road. But now that such marques as MV Agusta and Ducati are making super-expensive machines for production, Bimota's efforts have been overshadowed, and its bikes are now more noticeable for their quirky appearance than their state-of-the-art performance.

What makes the Tesi 3D stand out is its hub-centre steering, said to benefit handling because it eliminates fork flex under heavy braking, the force being transmitted through the frame instead. Alterations to the previous 2D's steering geometry make for quicker turning, but the new bike's most notable aspect is its extraordinary slimness. Bimota's designers claim it is the 'thinnest' large-capacity sports motorcycle available.

This bike is indeed extremely svelte and will no doubt be very uncomfortable over a long distance, although it isn't a machine built for distance but for short, hard blasts on the track and minor roads. For this reason it comes with race-style radial brake calipers that are unusually positioned – in true Bimota style – beneath the disc, to keep the mass as low as possible. Standard instruments include a lap timer and a computer that can record average and maximum speeds.

The 3D's most disappointing feature is its engine: the basic, Ducati-produced 1100-cc DS (Dual Spark) unit also used in the Monster and Multistrada. It yields just 71 kW (95 bhp), although the bike's lightness makes it seem much livelier than it does in more conventional machines.

Engine
1078 cc, 90-degree L-twin, eight-valve, four-stroke
Power
71 kW (95 bhp) @ 7750 rpm
Torque
103 Nm (76 ft lb) @ 4350 rpm
Gearbox
Six-speed
Final drive
Chain
Weight
168 kg (370 lb)
Top speed
209 km/h (130 mph) (est.)

CAGIVA MITO 500

Engine
510 cc, liquid-cooled, overhead-camshaft, single-cylinder, four-stroke
Power
45 kW (60 bhp) @ 7000 rpm (est.)
Torque
N/A
Gearbox
Six-speed
Final drive
Chain
Weight
135 kg (298 lb)
Top speed
193 km/h (120 mph) (est.)

When MV Agusta first launched its F4 750 back in 1998, I was lucky enough to be offered an early ride on the Gold Series edition made especially for Giovanni Castiglioni, son of MV owner Claudio Castiglioni. Afterwards I asked Giovanni what was his favourite motorcycle, and his reply came as a surprise: 'My tuned Cagiva Mito 125 – it's just such incredible fun to ride.'

Almost a decade later the crowds at the 2006 Milan Motorcycle Show were flocking to the Cagiva stand to see this fabulous concept bike: a Mito with a 500-cc engine, designed by Giovanni Castiglioni himself.

The Supermono racing class took off in Italy about twenty years ago, when riders began to build lightweight competition machines by fitting large-capacity, single-cylinder, four-stroke engines into 125-cc sports-bike chassis. Although the trend was started by amateur builders, the big factories followed suit, notably Ducati with its fabulous Supermono 500 of 1993 and Gilera with the Saturno. Sadly the class died out after a few years, but if Cagiva's half-litre Mito goes into production – and there seem to be enough potential buyers to make it viable – Europe's racetracks could once more be echoing to the drone of racing singles.

The Mito 500 unites a standard 125-cc frame and a Husqvarna 510 engine that produces 45 kW (60 bhp). With just 135 kg (298 lb) to propel, this is a fabulous marriage in terms of acceleration and, above all, handling.

Designed by Massimo Tamburini, creator of the legendary Ducati 916, the Mito 125 always looked like a miniature version of that machine. The iconic styling has been retained for the Mito 500, which is expected also to appear as a replica of the Grand Prix 500 that Cagiva campaigned during the early 1990s. Castiglioni has even hinted that a one-make race series might be formulated for the model.

Likely to be another attraction of the Mito 500 is its affordability. By sourcing certain ancillary parts from budget producers, Cagiva hopes to keep the retail price down to that of a 'cooking' commuter bike.

CAGIVA

DUCATI 1098

It may have been an improvement on its predecessor and enjoyed great success in World Superbike Racing, but there is little doubt that the outgoing 999 supersports machine proved to be a huge commercial error for Ducati. *Ducatisti* had long revelled in the fact that the 916 – and its upgraded offspring, the 996 and 998 – boasted lines that were hailed the world over as among the sexiest ever to grace a motorcycle. But they were appalled at the appearance of the ugly-duckling 999 that replaced it, and it was no surprise that many defected to other marques.

However, Ducati's latest offering in the sector should have them coming back in droves: the 1098 is not only a great performing motorcycle but also looks *almost* as gorgeous as the old 916 design and manages to combine state-of-the-art v-twin engineering with all the character and passion expected of an Italian thoroughbred.

The bodywork design unashamedly draws inspiration from the 916, in features such as the twin, underseat exhaust pipes, the single-sided swing arm and the narrow, rectangular headlamps, but the overall look has a modernity that makes the old machine seem very much a 'classic'. Initial colour schemes are red, yellow or black, and, at the time of writing, white and Italian *tricolore* versions are also on the cards.

Yet few people will buy a 1098 for its looks alone; their priorities will be performance and handling. With 106 kW (142 bhp) on tap and massive v-twin torque, this is a machine that is joyous on a racetrack or winding country road, its huge reserves of power catapulting it out of corners, even low down the rev range. Handling is sublime, thanks to dimensions more akin to a 600-cc machine than a litre-plus one, and, on the S and R versions, top-of-the-range Ohlins suspension front and rear. And nearly every road tester has described the braking power of this gem as eye-popping.

The 1098's most obvious competitor is Aprilia's RSV Mille, which in 2006 was simply the best Italian v-twin superbike on the market. That mantle has now returned to Ducati, for the 1098 is faster, more powerful, better-handling and better-looking than its rival. No doubt Aprilia's engineers are already working to remedy all of that.

Engine
1099 cc, double-overhead-camshaft, 90-degree v-twin, eight-valve, four-stroke
Power
106 kW (142 bhp) @ 9800 rpm
Torque
113 Nm (83 ft lb) @ 7800 rpm
Gearbox
Six-speed
Final drive
Chain
Weight
171 kg (377 lb)
Top speed
282 km/h (175 mph)

HONDA CBR125R

Engine
124 cc, liquid-cooled, overhead-camshaft, single-cylinder, four-stroke
Power
10 kW (13 bhp) @ 9500 rpm
Torque
9 Nm (7 ft lb) @ 6000 rpm
Gearbox
Six-speed
Final drive
Chain
Weight
119 kg (262 lb)
Top speed
113 km/h (70 mph)

Winning customer loyalty at the earliest possible stage is as important to motorcycle brands as it is to the manufacturers of cars, domestic appliances and most other mass-market goods, so although Honda's CBR125 is an entry-level machine, it is vital that anyone who buys one becomes a dyed-in-the-wool Honda fan. For today's 125 riders are likely to be tomorrow's buyers of the CBR600 and Fireblade.

With its output limited to 10 kW (13 bhp), to take account of the learner restrictions in force in some countries, the CBR125 is probably not much faster or better accelerating than, for example, its least expensive Chinese-built equivalent, so its sales success depends heavily on image. And that is why it has been made to look like a scaled-down replica of Honda's full-sized supersport machines through the use of similar colour schemes; a full, race-style fairing; and a high-mounted pillion perch.

Underneath, however, the technology is fairly basic: the engine is a variation of the tried-and-tested overhead-camshaft, single-cylinder, two-valve unit that Honda has been making for decades and, although neither the chassis nor the brakes has been through the intensive development programmes afforded to the high-end, 'full-sized' motorcycles, they are more than capable of coping with the CBR125's modest output and endowing the machine with decent handling.

This bike does have one important extra, however: the letter 'R', for 'racing', at the end of its model name, because at this level image is everything.

120
140
160
100
180
80
200
60
40
20
0
8
9
10
11
7
12
6
13
5
4
FI
3
2
1
0
E
F
C
H

HONDA

HONDA
RR

HONDA
CBR
HONDA

HONDA CBR600RR

Honda's long-running and ever-popular CBR600 was knocked off its perch in 2006 by the arrival of stunning middleweight machines from Suzuki and Yamaha. This latest RR version, however, puts the big H back at the front of the grid. Every year one wonders how much further Japan's engineers can take the 600-cc supersport category, and every year one or other of them produces a smaller, lighter, faster and often more useable machine.

Honda has achieved all four with the 600RR, by the simple expedient of changing, well, everything. The engine, frame and bodywork are all new, with perhaps the most significant improvement being in the first. One of the drawbacks of race-orientated machines of this capacity is the very thing that makes them thrilling to ride: they need to be revved relentlessly. That's fine when you're really going for it on a 'B' road or circuit, but a useful torque peak well below the red line is always desirable for real-world riding. Honda's technicians have managed to ensure that the 600RR pulls like a train from around 7000 rpm, which is little more than halfway through the available rev range, making it a delight for climbing hills and powering out of corners.

Handling is fabulously nimble, too, thanks to the fact that the frame has been 'shrunk' to a size that would not seem out of place on a bike of half this capacity. Indeed, this is a tiny motorcycle enveloped in a far smaller fairing than that of the old model, but ergonomics have been improved by extending the gap between seat and handlebar. There's less mass, too, thanks to the use of such lightweight components as titanium exhaust internals, and the engine alone is more than four pounds lighter than the old one, contributing significantly to a near-8kg (18 lb) weight loss.

An electronic steering damper also helps keep things on the straight and narrow, but features that are found on some of Honda's rivals, such as a racing-style slipper clutch and wireless throttle control, are missing. Such deficiencies do little, however, to diminish what is a fine machine.

Engine
599 cc, liquid-cooled, four-cylinder, 16-valve, four-stroke
Power
88 kW (118 bhp) @ 13,500 rpm
Torque
66 Nm (49 ft lb) @ 11,250 rpm
Gearbox
Six-speed
Final drive
Chain
Weight
155 kg (342 lb)
Top speed
265 km/h (165 mph)

KAWASAKI NINJA ZX-6R

Engine
599 cc, liquid-cooled, double-overhead-camshaft, four-cylinder, 16-valve
Power
93 kW (125 bhp) @ 14,000 rpm
Torque
60 Nm (44 ft lb) @ 11,700 rpm
Gearbox
Six-speed, cassette type
Final drive
Chain
Weight
167 kg (368 lb)
Top speed
265 km/h (165 mph)

Previously, if you wanted a ZX-6 for the street you bought the standard R model, or if you wanted one for competition on the track you bought the RR. But now Kawasaki has rolled the two into one to create yet another machine that offers blistering circuit performance yet is also sufficiently well mannered for the daily run to work.

Inspired by the Big K's mantra of 'Power, Performance, Exhilaration', and assessed throughout its development by a former Grand Prix racer, this is undeniably a cutting-edge performance machine. As with its rivals, the ZX-6R's engine is more compact than that of the model it replaces and, as with Honda's CBR600RR, emphasis has been placed on improving torque to make the bike more tractable both when gassing it out of a racetrack hairpin and when trickling through city traffic.

But the real delight of sport bikes of this capacity is screaming them up to the red line in every available gear to make maximum use of their prodigious top-end power. The ZX-6R doesn't disappoint, churning out 93 kW (125 bhp) at a heady 14,000 rpm. Sustained high revving is made possible by ultra-lightweight valve gear and a modified ECU (electronic control unit) that ensures that the engine receives precisely the correct amount of fuel vapour from the injection system at every throttle setting, allowing smooth running throughout the range.

The ZX-6R's race credentials are underlined by its close-ratio cassette gearbox (which, in competition use, can be quickly swapped for an alternative unit, depending on the type of track) and one of the best slipper clutches available on a production bike. An ultra-rigid, twin-spar aluminium frame keeps everything together, and an extended swing arm ensures excellent high-speed stability, while a new feature that Kawasaki calls a 'top-out spring' stops the back end from pattering excessively during hard braking.

The radial brakes and petal discs are as enormously powerful as they need to be, and, in line with current trends, the machine has been given a smaller fairing than the previous model in order to reduce drag.

Kawasaki
Ninja

Kawasaki
Ninja

F4 1080
F4

MV AGUSTA F4 1100 CC

This is expected to be the ultimate development of MV Agusta's F4 1100, which could already be described as the Ferrari of motorcycles, and, at more than £60,000, this limited-edition version is well on the way to having a Ferrari-sized price tag. The 'CC' in the title refers to the fact that this is a special edition designed by and named after MV's president, Claudio Castiglioni.

Bristling with state-of-the-art componentry, the F4 1100 CC has an upgraded, large-capacity engine with lightweight internals, variable inlet tracts, and an exhaust system made entirely of titanium. Crankshaft output is claimed to be an arm-wrenching 148 kW (198 bhp), putting the road-going F4 almost in the league of contemporary Grand Prix bikes and making it the most powerful production motorcycle ever built. All the bodywork is carbon fibre and the wheels are of forged aluminium, which helps keep the weight down to 187 kg (412 lb); less than half the weight of a Honda Gold Wing, yet the MV's engine produces 70 per cent more power.

The machine is expected to form the basis of MV Agusta's assault on the World Superbike Championship, in which it is scheduled to compete in 2008. Just one hundred F41100 CCs will be built, and each buyer will receive a hand-stitched Trussard leather riding jacket and a special-edition Jean Richard wristwatch that will be numbered to match the plaque fitted to the fork yoke of each motorcycle.

Castiglioni has given machine number one to his son, Giovanni, who is believed to have ordered a glass case in which to display the bike in his drawing-room.

Engine
1080 cc, liquid-cooled, double-overhead-camshaft, four-cylinder, 16-valve, four-stroke
Power
148 kW (198 bhp) @ 12,200 rpm
Torque
125 Nm (92 ft lb) @ 9000 rpm
Gearbox
Six-speed
Final drive
Chain
Weight
187 kg (412 lb)
Top speed
314 km/h (195 mph) (limited)

NCR MILLONA

Engine
Ducati 1200 NCR l-twin, eight-valve, four-stroke
Power
85 kW (114 bhp) @ 8450 rpm
Torque
N/A
Gearbox
Five-speed
Final drive
Chain
Weight
121 kg (267 lb)
Top speed
265 km/h (165 mph) (est.)

NCR is a motorcycle engineering company situated near Ducati's Bologna HQ that has established something of a reputation as the famous marque's unofficial tuning and racing development arm. It was founded in 1969 by Rino Caracchi and Giorgio Nepoti with the sole aim of upgrading Ducatis for racing, and that is pretty much what it has done ever since.

From humble beginnings tuning and modifying machines for club racing, NCR came to be recognized as the best in its field, and gradually attracted the respect of big-name riders. Before long the NCR team bikes were regarded as the benchmark for competitive Ducatis the world over, as they took the chequered flag at such major events as the Montjuic 24 Hours and the Mugello 1000 Kilometres.

NCR was bought in 2001 by the metal-processing company Poggipolini, which specializes in providing titanium, magnesium and special steels for use in Formula One, MotoGP and aeronautical and marine applications. Its president, Stefano Poggipolini, is a great fan of motorsport and set NCR on the road to becoming a producer, rather than just a preparer, of exclusive racing motorcycles.

In just two years, NCR has brought several track-only machines to production, the latest of which is the 2007 version seen here. Powered by a race-tuned version of the 1080-cc engine used in the Ducati Multistrada, the new Millona is an exquisitely crafted, lightweight machine that has a power-to-weight ratio almost equal to that of the most state-of-the-art Japanese superbikes. By using titanium fasteners throughout and lightening the gearbox, NCR has reduced the mass of the Ducati powerplant to a mere 50 kg (110 lb) while boosting its output by 10 per cent. The extra power has been released through a combination of NCR's own, specially profiled camshaft and a two-into-one-into-two exhaust system crafted from titanium.

MTECH
SUOMY
NCR

SIDI
ZARD

brembo

brembo

STEFFANO CAFÉ9

The received wisdom about the poor sales of Ducati's 999 sports bike is that it just wasn't good-looking enough. Well, here's a 999, and even the most discerning will surely agree that it's downright gorgeous.

This version is, of course, a 'special' created by award-winning custom-motorcycle builder Robert Steffano, who is known among wealthy collectors for making bespoke luxury bikes. But the Steffano Café9 is aimed at a wider public, for this is a production machine that will be built in sufficient numbers to satisfy demand.

Steffano takes a stock 999, throws away all the ugly bits, and re-dresses it with his own snub-nosed bikini fairing, a single-seat unit covered in stingray skin, and a hand-beaten aluminium exhaust system with exits at the sides of each silencer rather than at the back. This modern-day interpretation of a 1950s café racer also gets 20-spoke, forged-alloy wheels and an integrated system for detecting police radar.

While the new carbon-fibre fairing might not be as aerodynamic as Ducati's original, it certainly helps save weight, because the Café9 tips the scales at over 10 kg (22 lb) less than the stock bike. On a practical note, it retains Ducati's adjustable handlebars and footrests for ultimate riding comfort.

The Café9 is built in an eco-friendly workshop powered by a mini hydroelectric system and solar panels in the hills of northern California, and its test track is the Pacific Coast Highway. 'This is the real world, with real roads, and endless places to appreciate the awesome capabilities of these machines', Steffano says.

Engine
999 cc, liquid-cooled, l-twin, eight-valve, four-stroke
Power
Up to 111 kW (149 bhp) @ 9750 rpm, depending on tuning
Torque
115 Nm (85 ft lb) @ 8000 rpm
Gearbox
Six-speed
Final drive
Chain
Weight
170 kg (375 lb)
Top speed
241 km/h (150 mph)

SUZUKI GSX-R1000

Engine
999 cc, liquid-cooled, double-overhead-camshaft, four-cylinder, 16-valve
Power
139 kW (187 bhp) @ 12,500 rpm (est.)
Torque
N/A
Gearbox
Six-speed
Final drive
Chain
Weight
172 kg (379 lb)
Top speed
306 km/h (190 mph) (est.)

Like its main rivals, Honda, Kawasaki and Yamaha, with their competing machines, Suzuki has done much to improve the already superb GSX-R1000, which has for several years been a regular 'king of the sports bikes'. Naturally, the new model is even more powerful, and detail changes abound, from the number of minute holes in the fuel-injection nozzles (trebled to twelve) to the type of spark plugs that light the engine's fire (the latest are iridium-coated for better performance).

In keeping with the current obsession for engineering compactness, Suzuki has also fitted the GSX-R with vertically staggered transmission shafts to reduce front-to-rear engine length, while the close-ratio gearbox itself is married to an adjustable slipper clutch for smoother downshifts.

But perhaps the most interesting feature of the new machine is that the rider can control exactly how much of the engine's prodigious power he or she wants to apply, not just through the conventional means of using different throttle openings but also by taking advantage of an extremely powerful ECM (Engine Control Management) system. This makes it possible for one of three power settings to be selected, using a three-way switch mounted on the right handlebar.

The engine mapping varies with each setting, and each map was developed using experience gained building race-bike maps for rainy, mixed, or dry track conditions. Switching from one map to another is instantaneous, making it possible for a rider to select one map for one part of a racetrack and another map for another part. The system also allows the rider to select a different setting to suit conditions when tyre grip is reduced, or to choose one map for a high-speed racetrack and a different map for a tighter racetrack. Of course, all the settings are also available for road use.

Suzuki's lead will almost certainly be followed by other manufacturers before long; as might the marque's return to a twin-silencer set-up, the only one of its type currently seen on a Japanese four-cylinder supersports machine. The latest high-volume, titanium-and-stainless-steel version of the Suzuki Advanced Exhaust System (SAES) features equal-length head pipes that feed a collector, a short mid-pipe and a unique under-engine chamber that leads to the two stubby, aluminium-and-titanium silencers.

According to Suzuki, the addition of the under-engine chamber and the use of two low-slung silencers instead of one larger one together almost double exhaust internal volume while also lowering the centre of gravity, centralizing the mass, and increasing aerodynamic performance.

Among the bike's other interesting features are an electronically controlled steering damper and three-position adjustable footrests and foot control pedals.

This is said to be 'the most powerful and most efficient GSX-R ever built' in the model's twenty-two-year history, and in our opinion it's the best-looking, too.

SUZUKI

VYRUS 984 C3

If you've already read about the new Bimota Tesi 3D (see pp. 24–25), you may wonder why such a remarkably similar machine is featured here under the Vyrus name. The answer is that Vyrus was created by a former Bimota employee during one of the many periods when cash problems placed Bimota in 'suspended animation'.

Like the Bimota, the Vyrus uses Ducati power and is available as a 985 C3 version fitted with a 112-kW (150-bhp) engine from the 999. The 984 C3 seen here, however, makes do with the 74-kW (100-bhp) 1000 DS engine used in the Monster and Multistrada models. This new version is named 'Black Rocket' because all of its alloy components have been anodized black and its engine has been tuned to produce an additional 7 kW (10 bhp) over standard.

The Vyrus may look more like an artwork than a riding machine, but it was born out of its designer's interest in functionality rather than mere appearance. The frame is ultra-stiff and the steering very light and very sensitive, while front-to-rear weight distribution has been calculated to be almost perfect with an average-weight rider at the controls.

Compared with any mass-market Japanese sports bike, or even the Ducati on which it is based, the Vyrus is prodigiously expensive, but thankfully there are probably more buyers out there who are willing to pay to be different than there are riders willing to be converted to the benefits of motorcycles with hub-centre steering. Were it the other way around, such firms as Vyrus and Bimota might not exist at all. Long may both prosper.

Engine
991 cc, 90-degree l-twin, four-valve, four-stroke
Power
75 kW (100 bhp) @ 7750 rpm
Torque
103 Nm (76 ft lb) @ 4350 rpm (est.)
Gearbox
Six-speed
Final drive
Chain
Weight
168 kg (370 lb)
Top speed
209 km/h (130 mph) (est.)

YAMAHA YZF–R1

Engine
998 cc, liquid-cooled, double-overhead-camshaft, four-cylinder, 16-valve
Power
134 kW (180 bhp) @ 12,500 rpm
Torque
118 Nm (87 ft lb) @ 10,000 rpm
Gearbox
Six-speed
Final drive
Chain
Weight
177 kg (390 lb)
Top speed
301 km/h (187 mph)

Another year, another round of improvements in the one-litre sports-bike class. More power, lighter weight, quicker steering – it has all become rather predictable, but somehow each revision of a popular model makes the one that appeared so wonderful last year seem as though it belongs in the last century.

The 2007 Yamaha R1 might look very similar to the previous offering, but extensive engine tweaks have increased power by 4 kW (5 bhp) to 134 kW (180 bhp), although top speed has actually come down, if for no other reason than that the new version has been fitted with a top-gear rev limiter that prevents it from passing 301 km/h (187 mph) – which is enough for most of us.

As with some of the bikes in the 600-cc supersports class, Yamaha's engineers have paid a great deal of attention to making the flagship R1 more tractable and rider-friendly by improving the torque curve. They have even included a race-style 'launch control' system to help get the bike off the line as fast as possible without the need to waste valuable fractions of a second wrestling wheel spin or preventing the front end reaching for the sky.

Among other race-inspired equipment benefiting this machine is the YCC-T (Yamaha Chip Controlled Throttle), which does away with the old-fashioned cable method, and new four-valve cylinder heads fitted with titanium intake valves and designed along the lines of the YZR-M1 MotoGP bike. Handling is beyond excellent, thanks to a new set of upside-down, multi-adjustable front forks and firmer, better-damped rear suspension linked to a revised 'Deltabox' aluminium chassis.

Compare the new R1 with its rivals from Kawasaki, Suzuki and Honda, however, and there are several areas where it appears to lag behind. The Kawasaki ZX-10R, for example, offers slightly better roll-on from 161 km/h (100 mph), while the Honda Fireblade has a more even spread of torque and more low-down power. But the truth of the matter is that all these machines have for years been way beyond the capabilities of the average street rider. As a result, the choice now is more down to the brand with which a buyer feels the most affinity and which GP star he or she would most like to emulate.

YAMAHA

R1
YAMAHA

SUPERMOTO, TRAIL AND ENDURO

Aprilia's excellent Pegaso trail bike was made more road-biased in 2005, when it appeared in 'Strada' form, and then it was reinstated as a dual-purpose machine the following year, before now being offered in this special, more hard-core factory version.

With all Aprilias the use of the word 'Factory' denotes the addition of some exotic extra parts and, in most cases, a markedly higher price tag, but the remarkable thing about the Pegaso Factory is that the many desirable extras seem to have had little effect on the price, making it a real bargain compared with such rival machines as BMW's F650 GS.

So what do you get for your money (around £5000 in the United Kingdom)? Well, all the good things about the standard Pegaso, plus lightweight, gold-anodized, spoked wheel rims; a four-piston radial front-brake caliper matched to a radially mounted master cylinder; braided brake hoses; handlebars from Aprilia's Tuono naked bike; an architectural-looking handlebar clamp machined from a solid lump of aluminium; and several pieces of carbon-fibre bodywork. At extra cost you can even specify a pair of Akrapovic racing exhausts to help the liquid-cooled, single-cylinder engine breathe more easily and sing more loudly.

With typical Italian flair, Aprilia has managed to make the Pegaso Factory one of the best-looking motorcycles in its class, although the finish is of a standard more commonly associated with Japanese manufacturers than with European ones. All in all, this is an excellent, versatile and well-thought-out motorcycle.

APRILIA PEGASO FACTORY

Engine
659 cc, liquid-cooled, fuel-injected, single-cylinder, four-stroke
Power
36 kW (48 bhp) @ 6250 rpm
Torque
61 Nm (45 ft lb) @ 5200 rpm
Gearbox
Five-speed
Final drive
Chain
Weight
168 kg (370 lb)
Top speed
145 km/h (90 mph)

APRILIA RXV 450i/ 550i

Engine
449 cc; 549 cc, liquid-cooled, fuel-injected, 77-degree v-twin, four-stroke
Power
449 cc, 48 kW (64 bhp); 549 cc, 52 kW (70 bhp) @ 13,500 rpm
Torque
449 cc, 42 Nm (31 ft lb); 549 cc, 52 Nm (38 ft lb) @ 7000 rpm
Gearbox
Five-speed
Final drive
Chain
Weight
118 kg (260 lb)
Top speed
161 km/h (100 mph) plus

Aprilia's ultra-compact v-twin powerplant sparked a sensation in the enduro, supermoto and motocross worlds when it went into full production in 2006 as the engine used in such models as the RXV and SXV. But while the excellent power-to-weight ratio of these machines delighted accomplished off-road riders, it proved a little too much for the less experienced 'hobbyist'.

The latest RXV enduro bike is considerably more user-friendly, however, owing to some small alterations to its fuel-delivery system and an upgrade of the engine internals. The result is a motorcycle that an expert can ride even faster but one that is also fairly forgiving in the hands of a novice.

The modifications also mean that the RXV can be used just as effectively for gentle trail riding as it can for all-out racing. It has even been made sufficiently docile at low revs to be considered as a practical town bike: the smoothness and wide power spread of the engine make it far less 'snatchy' to ride than an equivalent-capacity single-cylinder machine.

If you really want to make the most of an RXV, it can be converted to a supermoto machine relatively easily with the addition of a pair of wheels from the SXV, which is essentially the same motorcycle but with the addition of a slipper clutch to reduce rear-wheel lock-up during sharp downward gear changes.

And full marks to Aprilia for making basic maintenance tasks easier to carry out by incorporating quick-release and hinged components for instant access to such areas as the air filter and throttle bodies.

BMW G650 XCHALLENGE/ XMOTO

The point of BMW's new G650 range is to attract further riders to the brand, but these bikes are also causing a stir among experienced off-road motorcyclists. The Xchallenge is a no-holds-barred forest racer with a huge amount of suspension travel front and rear and every possible component pared down for lightness.

This bike has the potential to be competitive straight from the crate, with its shatter-proof polypropylene bodywork, lightweight spoked wheels with aluminium hubs, weight-saving drilled brake discs and a low final-drive gear ratio that gives excellent acceleration and maximum low-speed flexibility.

The Xmoto (opposite and below, top right) is based on the same basic platform as the Xchallenge but in this case with a supermoto bias. The suspension set-up is entirely different, and the bike has 43.2-cm (17-in.) cast-aluminium wheels running on wide, super-tractable sports tyres for sharp handling on tarmac. The brakes, too, have been beefed up over those of the Xchallenge and the Xcountry (see pp. 98–99): the Xmoto gets a four-piston brake caliper and a 320-mm (12.6-in.) disc. And, to make it more suitable for highway use, the overall gearing is higher than that of the Xchallenge.

Engine
652 cc , liquid-cooled, double-overhead-camshaft, single-cylinder, four-valve, four-stroke
Power
40 kW (53 bhp) @ 7000 rpm
Torque
60 Nm (44 ft lb) @ 5250 rpm
Gearbox
Five-speed
Final drive
Chain
Weight
Xchallenge 144 kg (317 lb); Xmoto 147 kg (324 lb)
Top speed
Xchallenge 145 km/h (90 mph); Xmoto 169 km/h (105 mph)

CCM SR-40

Engine
398 cc, liquid-cooled, overhead-camshaft, single-cylinder, four-valve, four-stroke
Power
31 kW (42 bhp) @ 7000 rpm
Torque
39 Nm (29 ft lb) @ 5000 rpm
Gearbox
Five-speed
Final drive
Chain
Weight
128 kg (282 lb)
Top speed
145 km/h (90 mph)

The British company CCM has a reputation for producing quality off-road motorcycles that goes back over thirty-five years, and the new SR-40 continues this tradition with an interesting twist: although it is an entirely modern machine, it offers retro styling with its neat, alloy mudguards, polished fuel tank, headlamp stone guard and competition number boards. It is included in the Supermoto, Trail and Enduro section of this book, rather than among the Retro motorcycles, because, despite its 1970s looks, it is as competent a trail bike for today as any cutting-edge machine.

The liquid-cooled engine is supplied by Suzuki (it is the same as that used in the Japanese marque's top-selling DRZ400 enduro bike), and the SR-40's fairly light weight of 128 kg (282 lb) makes it easy to handle both on and off road. A special CCM exhaust system helps the engine breathe and sound better, while stopping is taken care of by front and rear disc brakes.

CCM is something of a phoenix risen from the ashes. Its previous owners put it into liquidation in 2004, only for it to be bought back less than a year later by Alan Clews, the man who originally set it up in 1971 and now runs it with his son and son-in-law.

PAIOLI

DERBI

DERBI

DERBI SENDA TERRA 125

Derbi's 'old' Senda trail bike was quite a hit with the youth of Europe and, despite its diminutive dimensions, it thoroughly proved its worth as a competent off-roader when a brace of Sendas completed Spain's Rally Baja Aragón without a single breakdown, even though they were the smallest machines in the field.

The Spanish manufacturer now appears to be returning to its off-road roots even more seriously with this latest version of the Senda Terra. As a result of a radical revamp, as well as being brought right up to date cosmetically, the bike has an all-new water-cooled engine with a four-valve cylinder head and anti-vibration balance shafts.

These modifications not only make the bike smoother to ride but also increase its power by 25 per cent over that of the previous model. A new frame and ancillary components make the bike lighter, too, so its all-round performance is markedly more lively. And, with plenty of ground clearance and a high-level exhaust pipe, the little Senda is certainly going to be just as useful off road.

There is more to come, too, because the advanced new engine is thought to have been designed so that it can form the basis of a more powerful, 200-cc version of the Terra that might even become available in full enduro guise.

Overall it is a good-looking machine, although the integrated headlamp and front mudguard unit seems to owe more than a hint of its design to BMW's GS range.

Engine
123 cc, liquid-cooled, overhead-camshaft, single-cylinder, four-valve, four-stroke
Power
11 kW (15 bhp) @ 8000 rpm
Torque
N/A
Gearbox
Six-speed
Final drive
Chain
Weight
105 kg (231 lb) (est.)
Top speed
113 km/h (70 mph)

DUSS SUPERMOTARD

If minimalism, superb engineering and imaginative design are high on the list of things you look for in a motorcycle, look no further than the radical Duss. Built in Switzerland by meticulous engineer Roland Duss, the Supermotard features a sculptural, in-house v-twin engine that forms a stressed member of the beautiful, handmade tubular frame.

The rear swinging arm adds to the minimal look, being of a round, s-shaped, single-sided construction that makes the back wheel of the bike appear to stand up of its own accord when viewed from the nearside. The bulbous fuel tank has cut-out air scoops – presumably to assist cooling of the giant, concave radiator mounted in front of it – and a small, twin-headlamp nose cone lends the bike a bug-like appearance.

Other neat touches include the old-fashioned 'bar end' rear-view mirrors and the almost seamless blending of the seat unit to the fuel tank. Quality components are used throughout the machine, including inverted front forks, radial brakes, a hydraulic clutch and Marchesini forged-alloy wheels.

Specifications not available

Husqvarna

super motard
CRC Technology

HUSQVARNA STR

Massimo Tamburini is well known as the designer of one of the best-loved motorcycles ever produced: Ducati's legendary 916 supersports machine. Now, however, he has turned his pen to creating a new breed of supermoto that boasts extreme versatility thanks to a remarkable adjustable frame.

Currently still at the concept stage, the Husqvarna STR is being billed as an 'urban supermoto' because its frame geometry can be pre-set to provide either lightning-fast turning ability (for competition use) or comfort and smoothness (for road riding).

The frame can be quickly and easily adjusted between the two modes by inserting a special tool into the central joint and turning it either clockwise or anti-clockwise to alter the angles of rake and trail. The frame itself is a sculptural blend of round and box-section aluminium tubing, and Tamburini has gone to great lengths to ensure that this will be a nimble machine with an excellent power- to-weight ratio. The STR should tip the scales at just 135 kg (298 lb), yet the 650-cc, water-cooled engine is expected to produce a class-leading 52 kW (70 bhp).

A fairly small, 13-litre (2.9 gallons) fuel tank should prove more than adequate for both race and urban use, while a lightweight digital-instrument pod and an ultra-compact exhaust system add to the bike's lithe looks.

Although the STR's frame seems radical, it is tipped to form the skeleton of a whole range of similar Husqvarna motorcycles and could even revolutionize the design of off-road racing machines, enabling their steering and turning to be adjusted to suit various types of terrain.

Engine
650 cc, liquid-cooled, fuel-injected, four-stroke
Power
52 kW (70 bhp) @ 10,000 rpm (est.)
Torque
N/A
Gearbox
Six-speed
Final drive
Chain
Weight
135 kg (298 lb) (est.)
Top speed
161 km/h (100 mph) plus

KTM 690 SM

Engine
653 cc, liquid-cooled, overhead-camshaft, single-cylinder, four-valve, four-stroke
Power
47 kW (63 bhp) @ 7500 rpm
Torque
65 Nm (48 ft lb) @ 6550 rpm
Gearbox
Six-speed
Final drive
Chain
Weight
152 kg (335 lb)
Top speed
177 km/h (110 mph)

KTM kept us on tenterhooks for quite a time over the replacement for its long-running and extremely popular 640 supermoto, but the wait has been worth it: not only is the 690 far more powerful and better handling, it is also markedly more radical-looking.

Engine output has been boosted considerably to 47 kW (63 bhp) from the 41 kW (55 bhp) of the 640 and it is relayed to the fat, 160-section rear tyre through an all-new six-speed transmission. But it is the bike's looks that have really caused interest among fans of both the KTM marque and of supermoto machines in general. From the beak-like front mudguard, which integrates with the headlamp assembly, to the tips of its rally-raid-style exhaust system, the new SM looks very different.

The marque's house colours of orange and black are enhanced by black anodized wheel rims, while the long, smooth seat is designed to take a pillion passenger if the machine is used for road riding, but also to make it easier for racing riders to reposition themselves quickly during the high-speed direction changes called for by supermoto.

The powder-coated chrome-molybdenum frame is equipped with exotic, race-standard suspension by White Power that comprises a rear monoshock and a set of inverted front forks, while the radial brake calipers are Brembo items, the front one acting on a giant, 320-mm (12.6-in.) drilled disc.

Although the SM comes equipped with lights, direction indicators, a horn and the other paraphernalia required to make it road legal, these parts are all designed to be easily removable if the bike is used for racing.

PRESTIGE

SUPERMOTO

KTM 950 SMR

You might well expect KTM's R version of its 950-cc 'monster' supermoto to be lighter, more powerful and better equipped than the standard model, but this is not the case. Instead, buyers of the R simply get an orange frame instead of a silver one, lots of black paintwork on everything from the bodywork to the wheels and the fork legs, and a slightly smaller-capacity fuel tank.

Although the changes are entirely irrelevant to the way the bike performs, there is no denying that the R looks meaner than its stablemates and, for that reason alone, it will attract buyers. The bike is not all show and no go, of course, because the v-twin engine still punches out 73 kW (98 bhp), quite enough to make the lightweight SMR huge fun to ride, with never-ending wheelies available in the first three gears.

Handling is superb, too, courtesy of taut White Power suspension front and back and fat, grippy tyres to complement the radially mounted Brembo brakes. But one of the bike's best features is the twin 'rocket-launcher' exhausts which rise menacingly from behind the engine.

Engine
942 cc, liquid-cooled, double-overhead-camshaft, v-twin, four-stroke
Power
73 kW (98 bhp) @ 8500 rpm
Torque
95 Nm (70 ft lb) @ 6500 rpm
Gearbox
Six-speed
Final drive
Chain
Weight
185 kg (408 lb)
Top speed
201 km/h (125 mph)

SACHS X-ROAD

Germany's oldest motorcycle manufacturer has collaborated with the Italian firm Morini Franco Motori to equip the latest version of the business-like X-Road with a brand-new, six-speed engine to make the most of its beautifully crafted trellis frame, neat, underseat exhaust pipe, giant front disc brake and sharp handling.

The X-Road offers considerable appeal to young riders thanks to its big-bike looks and a throaty exhaust note that belies the size of its engine. But its relatively high price tag means that buyers will really need to be looking for 'something different' if they are to choose it over one of its better-known Japanese rivals.

This is also one of those machines that might well be overlooked by more mature riders simply because of its capacity and the customer base at which it is aimed. Those more experienced motorcyclists who give the X-Road a try, however, will discover a machine that rewards with decent handling and superb in-town manoeuvrability. Fitted with trail-style wheels and tyres, it would also make a competent green-laner that is agile and light to pick up in the likely event of a spill.

Engine
124 cc, air- and oil-cooled, single-cylinder, four-stroke
Power
10 kW (13 bhp) @ 9000 rpm
Torque
N/A
Gearbox
Six-speed
Final drive
Chain
Weight
121 kg (267 lb)
Top speed
113 km/h (70 mph)

CRUISER

BIG DOG BULLDOG

Engine
1916 cc, overhead-valve, fuel-injected, v-twin, four-stroke
Power
N/A
Torque
N/A
Gearbox
Six-speed
Final drive
Belt
Weight
330 kg (728 lb)
Top speed
161 km/h (100 mph) (est.)

Big Dog Motorcycles of Wichita, Kansas, was founded as recently as 1994, but it is now the world's largest custom-bike manufacturer, having built more than 20,000 machines. The Bulldog was one of the original models, and this latest version takes the Big Dog ethos of wild looks even further than before, with its giant, 300-section rear tyre, curved frame tubes, 'diamond-cut' engine fins and a vast 197-cm (77.5-in.) wheelbase.

Like all Big Dog motorcycles, the Bulldog is powered by a hefty, 1900-cc, v-twin engine enhanced with components from specialist tuning house S & S and fitted with electronic fuel injection. The motor produces bags of low-down power, which is transmitted to the rear wheel through a hand-built, six-speed Baker gearbox.

For a decidedly exclusive machine – you are unlikely to return to your Big Dog to find another one parked beside it – the Bulldog and its brethren are surprisingly inexpensive, at around $34,000 in the United States, although this is more than double what you would expect to pay for a mass-produced factory custom bike from Japan.

Riding the Bulldog takes some getting used to, because of its excessive length. Corners should be approached with caution, and rather than allowing the bike to sweep around them in the conventional manner, a fair degree of concentration is required from the rider in order to compensate for the oversteer that is the price chopper riders pay for those eye-catching looks.

This bike is still built to be ridden, however, and to prove it Big Dog has fitted it with air suspension (note, by the way, how the rear shock absorbers have been cleverly concealed) and has even produced a range of practical, custom-made luggage to enable Bulldog owners to tour.

The neat, weather-resistant bag system has been designed to slip over the optional sissy bars so owners don't have to worry about ruining the machine's lines with unsightly racks or pannier frames. Other extras include high-performance exhaust systems with such names as 'Big Radius' and 'Mean Mother'. Could Big Dog be trying to convey a certain image?

HARLEY-DAVIDSON NIGHT ROD SPECIAL AND VRSCDX

Harley-Davidson's V-Rod models have almost become a brand within a brand, and a very successful one at that. These higher-tech, water-cooled alternatives to the traditional, somewhat agricultural Harleys that millions still adore have succeeded in proving beyond doubt that Milwaukee can produce motorcycles with modern power characteristics and aggressive performance.

The Night Rod Special puts a useful 90 kW (121 bhp) on to the road through its new, 240-mm-section rear tyre, and brings fresh meaning to the expression 'black looks' with its black engine, frame, forks and machined disc wheels. Its moody appearance is lightened only by the use of a little brushed steel on the exhaust system, but you do get a bit more decoration in the form of a pair of fuel-tank stripes: black on black denim or, if you want to be really different, black denim on black.

The limited-edition VRSCDX version of the Night Rod Special, created in honour of the successful V-Rod-based Screamin' Eagle/Vance & Hines NHRA Pro Stock drag racers, features a larger-capacity, more powerful engine, drag-style handlebars and fly screen, and a trick, flamed orange-and-silver paint job to give it the look of a street-legal racer. Just four hundred will be available worldwide.

Both models have been made more practical with the introduction of a longer-range, 18.9-litre (4.2-gallon) fuel tank, and they feature low-maintenance, carbon-fibre drive belts.

Engine
Night Rod Special, 1130 cc; Night Rod Special VRSCDX, 1250 cc; liquid-cooled, fuel-injected, double-overhead-camshaft, v-twin, four-stroke
Power
90 kW (121 bhp) @ 8250 rpm; 92 kW (123 bhp) @ 8250 rpm
Torque
108 Nm (80 ft lb) @ 7000 rpm; 116 Nm (85 ft lb) @ 7000 rpm
Gearbox
Five-speed
Final drive
Belt
Weight
291 kg (642 lb)
Top speed
225 km/h (140 mph); 233 km/h (145 mph)

HARLEY-DAVIDSON SOFTAIL CUSTOM FXSTC

Engine
1584 cc, fuel-injected, twin-camshaft, v-twin, four-stroke
Power
48 kW (65 bhp) @ 4500 rpm (est.)
Torque
125 Nm (92 ft lb) @ 3000 rpm
Gearbox
Six-speed
Final drive
Belt
Weight
305 kg (672 lb)
Top speed
185 km/h (115 mph) (est.)

Harley-Davidson developed its Softail range in 1984 in order to satisfy a demand for a rigid-framed, hard-tail chopper for, well, softies. Hidden from view beneath the bike's seat and rear-mudguard assembly is an upright rear shock absorber that enables the Softail to possess rigid-frame looks without the spine-jarring ride that is part and parcel of the real thing.

For many fans of the class, the long, low Softail has become the epitome of what a cruiser motorcycle should be, and Harley-Davidson has made the latest Custom FXSTC really look the part, with a polished, slotted disc rear wheel that is complemented by a traditionally spoked front. 'Ape hanger' handlebars, a small, bullet-style headlamp, a stepped seat with pillion backrest, and lashings of chrome complete the picture. All that needs to be added is a dark desert highway and the cool wind in your hair, as the Eagles might have said.

The most revolutionary aspect of this Softail, however, is the use of Harley's newly developed, twin-camshaft 96B engine, which is fed by electronic fuel injection and drives through a slick, six-speed gearbox. While still not as sanitized as the water-cooled powerplants used by the marque's Japanese counterparts, the 96B unit does make for a more refined machine. In fact, the models that have it are about as refined as most true Harley fans would ever want their bikes to be. Make everything too smooth and too easy and the all-important Harley-Davidson character might suddenly be lost. No one wants that to happen, because character is the very thing that ensures these bikes sell so well.

1200

With the possible exception of the Electra Glide, the Sportster is probably more synonymous with the Harley-Davidson brand than any other model. Being the firm's entry-level machine, a Sportster is the bike that many Harley enthusiasts start out on and, no matter how far they progress through the range, it invariably leaves them with good memories.

The original Sportster was launched in 1957, and although the model has undergone many changes over the decades – most notably the fitting of the rubber-mounted Evolution engine – it remains a no-frills machine designed to give simple riding pleasure and to provide a blank canvas, allowing an owner to develop a bike with a specific personality by adding accessories from the brand's huge parts catalogue.

This commemorative Sportster, produced with special paint and badging to mark the model's fiftieth anniversary, sticks to that ethos and otherwise looks very much the same as the previous model, but it is a very different machine in one respect: it has been dragged into the twenty-first century with the addition of electronic fuel injection.

This change, demanded in part by stricter emissions regulations, may sound simple enough to achieve, but it has called for a redesign of everything from the rear mudguard to the seat and from the fuel tank to the exhaust system. Even the frame has been altered.

The result is a smoother, easier-starting, more economical and marginally more powerful Sportster that still manages to retain its old character.

Other mod cons include a clock (how unrebellious is that?), a low-fuel warning light and dual trip meters. Harley also claims an 8 per cent reduction in the effort required to haul in the Sportster's formerly heavy clutch and, especially for those who immediately want to bolt a set of higher or wider handlebars to their new machine, 5 cm (2 in.) has been added to the switchgear wiring.

Electronic fuel injection now comes as standard on all Sportster models, including the base 883 versions.

HARLEY-DAVIDSON SPORTSTER 1200XL50 50TH ANNIVERSARY

Engine
1199 cc, air-cooled, fuel-injected, v-twin, four-stroke

Power
48 kW (65 bhp) @ 5500 rpm (est.)

Torque
107 Nm (79 ft lb) @ 4000 rpm

Gearbox
Five-speed

Final drive
Belt

Weight
253 kg (558 lb)

Top speed
177 km/h (110 mph)

HONDA SHADOW SPIRIT VT750DC

Engine
745 cc, liquid-cooled, v-twin, four-stroke
Power
34 kW (46 bhp) @ 5500 rpm
Torque
64 Nm (47 ft lb) @ 5500 rpm
Gearbox
Five-speed
Final drive
Shaft
Weight
229 kg (505 lb)
Top speed
161 km/h (100 mph)

Some aspiring motorcyclists dream of owning a large-capacity supersports model, others imagine riding through the wilderness on a trail bike, and some picture themselves disappearing into the sunset on a laid-back custom machine. It is the last group that the Shadow Spirit is aimed at: newly qualified riders who are more interested in image than in speed, performance or handling.

This latest incarnation of a design that can be traced back over twenty years is upgraded with the currently popular 53.3-cm (21-in.) front wheel and, in a more radical development, shaft drive instead of the former chain.

As with many cruisers , the VT750DC's designers have gone to some lengths to make the bike appear different from what it really is. Those fins on the engine imply that it is air-cooled, but in fact a slim radiator is tucked between the frame tubes, and while the front forks are made to look minimal and rather spindly, a sturdy brace to improve handling is hidden beneath the mudguard.

However, despite mechanical improvements over the old Shadow Spirit, such as that shaft drive and the use of twin-spark cylinder heads, the bike retains its basic braking equipment (a single front disc and a rear drum) and rudimentary suspension, which enables Honda to offer it at a remarkably competitive price.

Strictly speaking, cruiser-style motorcycles are not the best machines for new riders, but anyone whose heart is set on buying into this category would be hard-pressed to find something cheaper, more forgiving or easier to live with than this user-friendly Honda, which will undoubtedly continue to be a best-seller in its class.

HONDA

Kawasaki

KAWASAKI VN900 CUSTOM

There was a time when the only Japanese motorcycles that came equipped with a 53.3-cm (21-in.) front wheel were those designed for off-road use, but this is certainly not something for which Kawasaki's latest cruiser is suitable. The VN900's larger-than-usual front rim and raked-out fork give it a look that almost beats Harley-Davidson at its own game, a goal that every emulator of the iconic American marque secretly, or in many cases blatantly, wants to achieve.

For a mass-produced motorcycle, the VN900 (which has been named the Vulcan for the US market) does an accomplished job of imitating a one-off special. The combination of the large-diameter, cast-alloy, spoked front wheel and the fat, solid rear wheel, together with the minimalist headlamp and the smoothly sculpted fuel tank, give the impression that the bike's owner has been on a shopping spree at his local custom-parts outlet.

The heavily chromed engine also looks distinctly bespoke, as do the flat, drag-style handlebars on pull-back 'risers'. But to create a motorcycle such as this using individually sourced parts would cost much more than the modest £5600 that the VN900 retails for in the United Kingdom. It really is the epitome of a 'factory custom'.

A neatly concealed monoshock gives the machine the appearance of having a rigid rear end, further enhancing its bad-ass persona, but in reality it offers a ride that is smooth, comfortable and forgiving. The engine produces relatively little power for its capacity, but what it offers it delivers low down the rev range in classic cruiser style, making this the fastest-accelerating bike in its class and giving it excellent mid-range performance. Unusually for a cruiser, the VN900 is even quite practical, with a 290-km (180-mile) fuel-tank range, decent pillion accommodation and tolerable handling.

With 'customs' like this available to buy off the shelf, why bother to build your own for a lot more money?

Engine
903 cc, liquid-cooled, fuel-injected, v-twin, four-stroke
Power
40 kW (53 bhp) @ 4000 rpm (est.)
Torque
78 Nm (57 ft lb) @ 3700 rpm
Gearbox
Five-speed
Final drive
Belt
Weight
249 kg (549 lb)
Top speed
177 km/h (110 mph) (est.)

MOTO GUZZI 940 BELLAGIO

Moto Guzzi's new 940 looks almost too cool to be a factory-produced motorcycle, with its minimal, bobbed tail, flat, drag-style handlebars and deep saddle, yet it is. The manufacturer calls it a 'street roadster', and it was difficult to decide whether it belongs in the Cruiser or Street, Naked and Muscle section of this book because, in the purest sense, it is neither. For while it lacks the long, raked-out look of the first category, it is perhaps not sporty enough to compete with all-comers in the other.

Presented at Italy's 2007 EICMA show in Milan wearing a mean matt-black paint job, the 940 seems to be a direct competitor to such machines as Harley-Davidson's retro Nightster and Triumph's laid-back Speedmaster, but the shaft drive makes it a little more practical than either, and its 90-degree v-twin engine and sculptural exhaust plumbing give it further unique appeal.

Indeed, the more you look at the 940, the more its chameleon-like nature begins to emerge. Its rear tyre, for example, is fat enough to be stylish but not so vast as to impair handling; likewise, the rake of the fork is steep enough to provide a cruiser look but not so steep that the front will 'tuck in' during spirited bend-swinging. The rear-biased footrest position, too, makes this more of a 'rider's' motorcycle than the average cruiser and, as Moto Guzzi's marketing material rather floridly puts it, 'the bike seems glued to the ground but ready to take off at breathtaking speed'. So perhaps what we're really looking at is the world's first custom-cruiser-retro-sports bike?

Specifications not available

NHRA
DRAG RACING

SUZUKI M1800 R/RN/C INTRUDER

The last time I heard a bike manufacturer claim that it had built an engine containing pistons larger than those found in any other car or motorcycle was at the launch of Honda's giant VTX1800 cruiser in 2001. It took until 2006 for Suzuki to trump Honda, with the M1800, which has a slightly lower cubic capacity but, at 112 mm (4.4 in.), a bore 11 mm (0.4 in.) wider, meaning its pistons are the biggest yet.

The M1800 is probably the hottest-performing sports cruiser on the market, with those big pistons punching out 92 kW (123 bhp) and raising 160 Nm (118 ft lb) of torque. But such figures are almost essential in a motorcycle that weighs more than 340 kg (750 lb) fuelled up, especially when the rear tyre is 240 mm (9.5 in.) wide.

Despite its size, the M1800 accelerates rapidly, handles decently and stops quickly, mainly thanks to its sports-bike-style radial brakes and inverted front forks. No wonder, then, that Suzuki has been experimenting with alternative styles for the machine in order to broaden its market appeal. While the standard model has a menacing, hooded headlight, the RN version has a more traditional front end, and the C is more conservative still, with pure cruiser (rather than 'drag cruiser') looks and a stepped seat that offers greater passenger comfort than the somewhat apologetic perch that, on the R version, can be covered with a removable cowl. To describe any member of the trilogy as 'understated', however, might be going a little too far.

Engine
1783 cc, liquid-cooled, fuel-injected, v-twin, eight-valve, four-stroke
Power
92 kW (123 bhp) @ 6200 rpm
Torque
160 Nm (118 lb ft) @ 3300 rpm
Gearbox
Six-speed
Final drive
Shaft
Weight
340 kg (750 lb)
Top speed
225 km/h (140 mph) (est.)

VICTORY HAMMER S

Engine
1634 cc, air- and oil-cooled, fuel-injected, v-twin, four-stroke
Power
63 kW (85 bhp) @ 5500 rpm
Torque
136 Nm (100 ft lb) @ 3500 rpm
Gearbox
Six-speed overdrive
Final drive
Belt
Weight
299 kg (659 lb)
Top speed
193 km/h (120 mph)

The use of the letter 'S' at the end of this model's name points to the fact that here is a motorcycle with a little more performance than the average machine in the cruiser category. With a six-speed, overdrive gearbox, twin Brembo brake calipers, in excess of 1600 cc on tap and a set of inverted front forks that wouldn't look out of place on a sports bike, the new Hammer is clearly designed to bruise as well as cruise.

The sporty image is enhanced by a pair of red, powder-coated wheels, a blacked-out engine with polished cooling fins, a tachometer and a removable cowl to cover the pillion seat. The Freedom v-twin engine is of Victory's own design, while the massive rear tyre, with its 250-mm (9.8-in.) section – for a while the largest ever to be fitted to a production motorcycle – had to be specially developed by Dunlop.

The year 2008 marks Victory's tenth anniversary as a motorcycle manufacturer. In that relatively short time the company has developed a diehard following among riders who want something a little different from what is offered by America's 'other' maker of v-twin cruisers, and it is difficult to deny that such machines as the Hammer S and other bikes in Victory's range provide it.

HAMMER

VICTORY VEGAS 8-BALL

Black is certainly back when it comes to cruisers, and this explains the appearance of the Vegas 8-Ball, which takes its name from the one black ball found on a pool table. Black bodywork, fork sliders, triple clamps, handlebars and wheels make this a menacing and sleek machine that emphasizes its role as a cruiser for the lone wolf by having a single, banana-shaped saddle and no provision whatsoever for a passenger.

The lack of chrome, colour and cosmetic enhancement keeps the 8-Ball's price at the bottom of the Victory list, but you still get just as much motorcycle for your money, including the same gutsy, 1634-cc, fuel-injected engine that gives the entire range the edge in the performance-cruiser market.

In fact, the saving you'll make should leave enough cash left over to equip yourself with some of Victory's excellent branded riding gear. You might want to draw the line at the leather chaps, though: you can take this 'iron horse' business a bit too far.

Engine
1634 cc, air-cooled, fuel-injected, v-twin, four-stroke
Power
63 kW (85 bhp) @ 5500 rpm
Torque
136 Nm (100 ft lb) @ 3500 rpm
Gearbox
Six-speed overdrive
Final drive
Belt
Weight
299 kg (659 lb)
Top speed
193 km/h (120 mph)

Many easy-riding purists still believe that a true cruiser should be mechanically raw, loud and traditional in appearance. But it is a fact that many of the people who are looking for a motorcycle of this style are not in the first flush of youth and often want a tamer machine that is quieter and more refined than the type of mount that the typical road rebel might choose.

It is for just such riders that Yamaha has developed the XVS 1300, which offers an engine capacity and a physical presence to compare with anything in its class; it also has the additional 'luxuries' of a whisper-quiet, counterbalanced, water-cooled powerplant, smooth fuel injection, a catalytic-converter exhaust system and clean, low-maintenance belt drive.

Strict new emissions regulations have inevitably given significant impetus to the introduction of such improvements. The spin-off for the cruiser owner is that the machine becomes more pleasant and less tiring to ride and often more versatile. In the case of the XVS 1300, a further benefit is that the model is also available in 'touring' guise.

This machine is an excellent choice for relaxed, long-distance motorcycling, thanks to the lazy nature of the engine, the comfort provided by a long wheelbase, and a generous fuel capacity of 20 litres (4.5 gallons), which is made possible by the use of a twin-tank system. Footboards come as standard, but one of the most distinctive features of the XVS 1300 is its peculiar, bulbous headlamp, which, the manufacturer claims, lends it a 'wild, streamline style'.

YAMAHA XVS 1300A MIDNIGHT STAR

Engine
1304 cc, liquid-cooled, fuel-injected, v-twin, four-valve, four-stroke

Power
54 kW (73 bhp) @ 5500 rpm

Torque
78 Nm (57 ft lb) @ 3700 rpm

Gearbox
Five-speed

Final drive
Belt

Weight
249 kg (549 lb)

Top speed
177 km/h (110 mph)

ADVENTURE SPORTS

MM3
brembo

BENELLI AMAZONAS 1130

Engine
1130 cc, liquid-cooled, fuel-injected, v-twin, four-stroke
Power
92 kW (123 bhp) @ 9000 rpm
Torque
115 Nm (85 ft lb) @ 6250 rpm
Gearbox
Six-speed
Final drive
Chain
Weight
205 kg (452 lb)
Top speed
209 km/h (130 mph)

With sales in the adventure-sports sector remaining steady the world over, there are few marques that don't want to produce a large, comfortable, go-anywhere motorcycle that can win them a slice of the action. Benelli is the latest to get in on the act with its aggressively styled Amazonas, which looks more than a match for such rivals as the BMW R1200 GS Adventure and, most notably, the Triumph Tiger.

Until now the Tiger has been the only three-cylinder bike in this category, so the Amazonas triple presents some serious competition. The three-cylinder format works well in this sort of machine, as it makes for an effective compromise between the torque of a twin – useful for low-speed riding on tricky terrain – and the motorway-eating capabilities of a four.

The standard adventure-sports requirements are all there on the Amazonas: a commanding, upright riding position; physically large dimensions for relaxed long-distance cruising; and a fairing that is effective enough to prevent buffeting at motorway speeds but also small enough not to be too obtrusive for off-road use. A 21-litre (4.6-gallon) fuel tank should give the bike a range of more than 320 km (200 miles) between refills, while other practical touches include the handlebar brush guards and spoked wheels, which take more resolutely to an off-road battering than do the cast variety. Grippy, all-terrain tyres come as standard.

With great looks and performance to match, the Amazonas is likely to give Benelli's rivals something to worry about.

Benelli
EXCEL

BMW has produced some excellent motorcycles across the board during recent years, but the new X range of bikes looks set to provide the marque with one of its greatest sales successes. The other two models in the series are discussed in the Supermoto, Trail and Enduro section of this book, but the Xcountry doesn't quite belong there as it is less of an extreme off-road machine (see pp. 54–55).

Compared with the large-capacity overlanding motorcycles that we have become used to in this category, the Xcountry looks tiny – possibly too tiny to be considered appropriate for serious distance work. But anyone who remembers the dawn of the overlanding craze back in the early 1980s will know that one of the most popular machines among hardened two-wheeled travellers was Yamaha's XT 600.

Correctly kitted-out with appropriate luggage, XTs were ridden around the world from every starting point imaginable. The light, agile Xcountry lends itself to the same sort of major expeditions, thanks to the fact that it combines obvious off-road potential with enough of a bias towards road use to make it sufficiently comfortable for eating up huge distances.

It won't be long before the producers of after-market accessories are designing equipment that will make the Xcountry the bike to be seen on among committed overlanders, for this is a Yamaha XT 600 for the twenty-first century.

BMW G650 XCOUNTRY

Engine
652 cc, liquid-cooled, double-overhead-camshaft, four-valve, four-stroke
Power
40 kW (53 bhp) @ 7000 rpm
Torque
60 Nm (44 ft lb) @ 5250 rpm
Gearbox
Five-speed
Final drive
Chain
Weight
148 kg (326 lb)
Top speed
169 km/h (105 mph)

DUCATI MULTISTRADA 1100S

Engine
1078 cc, l-twin, eight-valve, four-stroke
Power
70 kW (95 bhp) @ 7750 rpm
Torque
103 Nm (76 ft lb) @ 4750 rpm
Gearbox
Six-speed
Final drive
Chain
Weight
196 kg (432 lb)
Top speed
209 km/h (130 mph)

Ducati declared its Multistrada – 'the motorcycle for all roads' – to be a revolution when it was launched in 2003, but, after a few years of strong sales, interest began to flag, and it became obvious that this quirky-looking bike needed a fillip. Ducati's answer was to give it a larger, 1078-cc engine for a bit more 'oomph' (not that it needed it) and to introduce this top-of-the-range S version.

The Multistrada S is equipped with the best-quality racing suspension front and rear from the Swedish firm Ohlins, and is dressed up with lots of expensive carbon-fibre goodies, such as a front mudguard and cam-belt covers. For the extra money that the S costs, you also get a set of beautifully engineered, tapering handlebars and black-painted wheels. Other than that, the bike is pretty much the same as the standard model.

The S has unfeasibly sharp handling for a machine with such an upright stance, and it really is a hoot to ride on twisty roads.

Those 'unusual' looks have, however, proved to be a bit off-putting to many potential buyers, so it is only a matter of time – and probably quite a short time at that – before we see an all-new Multistrada. But it will have to be good, as the competition has hotted up considerably since the launch of the original.

DUCATI
DUCATI

HONDA

HONDA

HONDA VARADERO 125

Pull up alongside Honda's baby Varadero and you might not realize that the engine that powers it is of a mere 125-cc displacement because, for all its learner-legal status, this machine has big-bike looks and lots of style.

Intended as an entrée into the world of adventure-sports motorcycling, the Varadero 125 also makes an excellent urban commuter, owing to its comfortable, upright riding position, superb manoeuvrability and frugal fuel consumption. The engine, which is very sophisticated for its size, being a liquid-cooled v-twin, has now been updated with electronic fuel injection that enables a gallon of fuel to be stretched for up to 201 km (125 miles). Combine this with the Varadero's generous tank and it is possible to travel more than twice that distance between refuelling stops.

If you are prepared to put up with a comfortable cruising speed of 80–100 km/h (50–62 mph), this really would make an excellent bike for long-distance touring on smaller roads and exploring the wilderness. Unlike its 1000-cc big cousin, the 125 is a featherweight and therefore easy to keep control of on rough surfaces and, in the event of a spill, equally easy to pick up.

There is ample space for two people, and the well-designed new fairing is as effective as it is attractive. And, just as there are with most full-sized adventure-sports bikes, plenty of accessories are available with which to customize your Varadero, ranging from a useful centre stand to an engine protection plate, electrically heated handlebar grips and a capacious top box. This is a truly practical machine.

Engine
125 cc, liquid-cooled, v-twin, eight-valve, four-stroke
Power
11 kW (15 bhp) @ 11,000 rpm
Torque
10 Nm (7 ft lb) @ 8500 rpm
Gearbox
Five-speed
Final drive
Chain
Weight
152 kg (335 lb)
Top speed
129 km/h (80 mph)

HONDA VARADERO XL1000V

Engine
996 cc, liquid-cooled, double-overhead-camshaft, v-twin, four-stroke
Power
70 kW (94 bhp) @ 7500 rpm
Torque
99 Nm (73 ft lb) @ 6000 rpm
Gearbox
Six-speed
Final drive
Chain
Weight
238 kg (525 lb)
Top speed
209 km/h (130 mph)

Honda's Varadero, which is named after a Cuban beach, has been around since 1999. It does not have the cult following of other adventure-sports machines, such as those produced by KTM or BMW, but if you want an affordable, ultra-reliable motorcycle for long-distance use, you will be hard-pressed to find one that does the job any better.

During its lifespan the Varadero has been subjected to numerous detail improvements that each time make it just that little bit more refined. This latest take on the model gets a redesigned screen that is more effective at motorway speeds; a new, more comfortable split seat; anti-lock braking and other useful features, such as a fuel gauge that displays 'remaining riding distance'.

The old plastic bash plate has been replaced by a sturdier aluminium one that should prevent all but the largest of rocks from damaging the underside of the engine, and the fairing has been equipped with handy pockets for carrying such items as passports and toll tickets. But the most sensible feature of all is the huge, 25-litre (5.5-gallon) fuel tank, which should give the Varadero a touring range of up to 402 km (250 miles), even allowing for the fact that large-capacity, v-twin engines are not renowned for their excellent fuel economy.

A range of sophisticated paint finishes indicates that this machine is not expected to indulge in too much off-road rough and tumble, as does the capacious, colour-matched pannier system, which can be ordered with a set of protective fabric covers. Hard-core overlanders may be tempted to opt for a BMW or KTM for their journey of a lifetime, but a Varadero fitted with the right set of tyres is probably no less capable off road than any of its equally hefty rivals, despite the fact that it is considerably cheaper. If I were planning a round-the-world trip and trying to save on costs, this would be a definite contender as my means of transport.

HONDA

REPSOL
3
REPSOL
euromilhões
3
REPSOL
MICHELIN
REPSOL

TYROLIT
TYROLIT
7
Vee Rubber

KTM 690 RALLY RAID REPLICA

If run-of-the-mill adventure-sports bikes are a little tame for you, perhaps the wild-looking KTM 690 Rally Raid Replica will be more up your street. If so, the chances are you won't remain friends with your neighbours for very long, because this motorcycle is a no-compromise desert-stormer with a bark as loud as its bite.

Designed to look and perform just like the factory racers that compete in such gruelling events as the Paris–Dakar Rally, the KTM 690 has a massive fuel tank, high-rise exhaust pipes, knobbly, go-anywhere tyres, and slippery bodywork that makes it easy for a rider to move around so as to get optimum balance in high-speed, off-road situations.

Further evidence of the Rally Raid's competition pedigree can be seen in that device poking up in front of the handlebars. A combined trip meter and route planner, it makes it easier to ensure that you are travelling the right way in the right time during a desert race or enduro. The Rally Raid has nothing superfluous whatsoever; everything on this motorcycle is there for one reason: to make it go as fast as possible over almost any terrain. It is available in a range of authentic team colours, including those of Red Bull Racing, Gauloises and Repsol.

The bike has been marketed by KTM to answer a growing demand for off-the-shelf rally-raid machines as more and more people take up the sport. And at present the Austrian manufacturer appears to be meeting that demand almost single-handedly: of the 250 entrants in the 2007 Paris–Dakar, no fewer than 128 chose KTM machines.

Engine
653 cc, liquid-cooled, single-cylinder, four-stroke
Power
45 kW (60 bhp) (est.) @ 9000 rpm
Torque
N/A
Gearbox
Six-speed
Final drive
Chain
Weight
140 kg (309 lb) (est.)
Top speed
177 km/h (110 mph)

KTM 990 SUPERDUKE

Engine
999 cc, liquid-cooled, fuel-injected, v-twin, eight-valve, four-stroke
Power
88 kW (120 bhp) @ 9000 rpm
Torque
100 Nm (74 ft lb) @ 7000 rpm
Gearbox
Six-speed
Final drive
Chain
Weight
186 kg (410 lb)
Top speed
217 km/h (135 mph) (est.)

Remember the *Mad Max* films, full of crazy-looking cars and equally crazy-looking motorcycles being ridden at death-defying speeds through a lawless landscape? Well, if it's time for a remake then the outlaws ought to be equipped with KTM Superdukes as the twenty-first-century alternative to the Kawasakis that were ridden in the first 'MM' movie of 1980.

Although we have included the Superduke in the Adventure Sports section of this book, it is perhaps in a class of its own. Part supermoto, part street fighter, part naked, who knows where it really belongs, other than on an endless ribbon of jet-black road, preferably without another vehicle in sight? Buy one of these bikes and we defy you not to ride it like a hooligan: the massive v-twin torque makes for the sort of stomp that encourages throttle-happy behaviour and rewards you with a laugh-inducing ride.

Once a small manufacturer of off-road competition motorcycles, KTM is now Europe's second-largest builder of powered two-wheelers, selling around 85,000 machines last year. Despite this pre-eminence, the company's products still have an air of originality about them that is exactly what many motorcyclists are seeking in an increasingly homogenized world.

In just a few short years of producing road-going motorcycles – its first road-biased product, the Duke 1, was launched in 1995 – KTM has established itself as an instantly recognizable brand, partly thanks to its striking black-and-orange colour scheme but also because of a distinctive look that is reminiscent of the 'form follows function' approach to industrial design, which took root in Europe in the early twentieth century.

And 'functional' certainly describes the Superduke: hard-wearing, black-coated components abound, from the five-spoke wheels to the fork tubes; the fuel tank is made from dent-proof polyurethane; and the handlebar area is uncluttered, allowing an unobstructed view of the road ahead. All in all, this bike means business.

Moto Morini
PIRELLI

Moto Morini, a brand that was revived in 2005, got off to a shaky start with its first Corsaro models, which attracted criticism for their poor ground clearance, snatchy throttle response and stiff gearboxes. But the fledgling firm rectified the problems and produced a far better-finished machine that is now achieving decent sales in Europe.

Unlike many reborn marques, Moto Morini is not using a bought-in engine but an in-house one built by its sister company, Morini Franco Motori. Best of all, the engine is designed by Franco Lambertini, who developed the 350-cc engine that powered Moto Morini's Sport and Strada models of the 1970s. It's a smooth, torquey unit that lends itself well to the first new Morini model, the naked Corsaro, but it could prove even better if it finds its way into this attractive-looking concept bike, the MM3. This is a direct competitor to Ducati's Multistrada, Yamaha's TDM 850 and even the class-leading BMW R1200 GS.

Based on the frame and mechanicals of the Corsaro 1200 naked, the MM3 is given an adventure-sports feel by longer travel suspension, better ground clearance, higher handlebars and a neat, wrap-around bikini fairing. The meaty, 1187-cc Corsaro unit has been detuned, but only very slightly, so the MM3 should still boast enough power to give thrilling corner-to-corner acceleration and endless wheelie-popping capability.

For all its fun-filled nature, this bike is a technical tour de force: traction control is standard, and throttle control is carried out by a cableless 'fly-by-wire' electronic device. The MM3 has anti-lock brakes and is expected to be offered with a full range of luggage options.

MOTO MORINI MM3

Engine
1187 cc, liquid-cooled, v-twin, eight-valve, four-stroke
Power
92 kW (123 bhp) @ 8250 rpm (est.)
Torque
120 Nm (88 ft lb) @ 6250 rpm (est.)
Gearbox
Six-speed
Final drive
Chain
Weight
190 kg (419 lb) (est.)
Top speed
209 km/h (130 mph)

TRIUMPH TIGER

Engine
1050 cc, liquid-cooled, fuel-injected, three-cylinder, four-stroke
Power
85 kW (114 bhp) @ 9400 rpm
Torque
100 Nm (74 ft lb) @ 6250 rpm
Gearbox
Six-speed
Final drive
Chain
Weight
198 kg (437 lb)
Top speed
217 km/h (135 mph)

The 'Tiger' name has been part of Triumph culture for decades, having been given at various times to both road-only and dual-purpose motorcycles. The reborn Triumph brand produced its first Tiger model in 1993, a 900-cc 'big trail bike' that was seen by overlanders as an interesting alternative to the more conventional BMW GS. Since then the Tiger has undergone a gradual metamorphosis, to the point where this latest version has the silhouette of an adventure-sports bike but not much off-road capability, although this is not to say that the Tiger has lost its bite.

Triumph has clearly discovered that most motorcycles in this category are used either for commuting or as a less cumbersome alternative to the standard 'full-dress' tourer. That is to say, they are required to cover long distances at high speed, usually with a pillion passenger and invariably with a hefty load of luggage. Relatively rarely do they venture into difficult off-road situations – so why compromise? Why not make a motorcycle with all the size and comfort of an adventure-sports machine but with more of an on-road bias?

The new-generation 'urban-sports' Tiger therefore has 43.2-cm (17-in.) cast-alloy wheels, a sleek fairing and standard road tyres. There is no underslung bash plate to protect the engine or the exhaust system, the seat is comfortably low and the suspension is far firmer than that of a trail bike, to make the most of the machine's on-road handling, which is impressive thanks to the beautifully engineered, lightweight aluminium frame.

Colour-matched luggage systems, demountable GPS and other touring accessories are also available.

TOURER AND SPORTS TOURER

BMW

BMW

BMW K1200R SPORT

BMW has certainly made the most of its ultra-powerful K1200 four-cylinder engine. The unit started life in the K1200S sports tourer, then appeared in the K1200R naked before being used in the full-dress K1200LT and then the only slightly smaller K1200GT. If you thought there couldn't possibly be another variation on the theme, you were wrong, because here we present the K1200R Sport, a machine that falls midway between the naked R and the fully faired S.

For my money this is the bike that works the best of the lot. Despite still being a large, heavy machine, it manages to look lithe and nimble thanks to the half fairing and neat back end, with its tucked-in, high-level exhaust pipe, yet the aerodynamics are still good enough to make it possible for a rider to hang on all the way up to the K's top speed of 270 km/h (168 mph) – something that's rather difficult to do on the naked R.

Unlike the competition, in the form of similar bikes from Aprilia, Benelli (Italy) and KTM (Austria), the BMW is not a machine on which to perform stunts; it is simply too heavy, partly because of its shaft drive. When it comes to real-world riding, however, it eats its rivals for breakfast because it handles superbly, has bags of power and, in true, practical, BMW style, is extremely comfortable over long distances.

And, as with all BMWs, there's a huge options list – everything from heated handlebar grips to an extra-wide rear wheel, and from electronic suspension adjustment to anti-lock brakes. Bikes in this category don't come more versatile.

Engine
1157 cc, liquid-cooled, double-overhead-camshaft, four-cylinder, 16-valve, four-stroke
Power
113 kW (152 bhp) @ 9200 rpm
Torque
130 Nm (96 ft lb) @ 7750 rpm
Gearbox
Six-speed
Final drive
Shaft
Weight
215 kg (473 lb)
Top speed
270 km/h (168 mph)

KAWASAKI 1400GTR

Engine
1352 cc, liquid-cooled, double-overhead-camshaft, four-cylinder, four-stroke
Power
127 kW (170 bhp) @ 11,500 rpm (est.)
Torque
155 Nm (114 ft lb) @ 8000 rpm (est.)
Gearbox
Six-speed
Final drive
Shaft
Weight
227 kg (500 lb) (est.)
Top speed
282 km/h (175 mph) plus

Back in the late 1980s, Kawasaki produced a large, heavy, road-munching tourer called the GTR1000. It was not hugely successful, and the model faded from the line-up as quietly as it had arrived. But now the letters 'GTR' have been revived for an all-new, long-distance machine that, according to Kawasaki, heralds the creation of a previously unknown category of motorcycle: the Transcontinental Supersport.

Imposing, fast, stable and supremely comfortable, the new GTR is built for the type of rider whose idea of a long weekend break is to jump on a bike in London and blast down to the south of France in a single hit, treating speed limits at his or her own discretion. Based on the hugely powerful ZZ-R1400 sports tourer featured in *The New Motorcycle Yearbook 2*, the GTR becomes a fully fledged tourer by virtue of its extra features designed to improve long-distance capability, among which are the largest headlamps and rear-view mirrors ever fitted to a production motorcycle.

Streamlined and integrated panniers come as standard with the 1400GTR, as does an electrically operated, height-adjustable windshield. There is even a copious glove-box built into the fuel tank. A four-part Tetra-Lever shaft-drive system has been designed to reduce transmission snatch to an absolute minimum, ensuring the smoothest possible progress. To pull this giant down safely from its top speed of almost 290 km/h (180 mph), race-quality, radially mounted brakes are provided, and these can be specified with or without an anti-lock system.

Mindful of the fact that this motorcycle is intended for sustained high-speed travel over great distances, Kawasaki has incorporated a comprehensive instrument panel display linked to a pair of pressure sensors that warn the rider of the slightest tyre anomaly.

Another high-tech feature borrowed from the automotive world is known as Ki-Pass, or Kawasaki Intelligent Proximity Activation Start System. This does away with fumbling in the pocket of a bulky riding suit for an old-fashioned ignition key, as the Ki-Pass electronic chip, which is carried by the rider, is uniquely coded to switch on the ignition once it is close enough to the machine.

Kawasaki
Kawasaki
ABS

norge

MOTO GUZZI NORGE 850

Among the new arrivals announced in *The New Motorcycle Yearbook 2* was the Moto Guzzi Norge 1200 touring machine, named after the touring bike built by Giuseppe Guzzi in the late 1920s, on which he rode from his base at Mandello del Lario in northern Italy all the way to the Norwegian Arctic Circle.

The Norge 1200 has been enjoying moderate success in a touring market that has, for some years, been dominated by BMW, so now the Italian firm has added an 850-cc version to the line-up. Why? Well, probably because bigger is not always better, or at least not to every rider. In many cases a smaller-capacity engine makes a motorcycle more pleasant to live with, even if it might be a little slower.

The simple fact that there is less reciprocating mass in a smaller motor can make it sweeter and crisper and, in the case of a touring machine such as the Norge, there will be an additional benefit in terms of fuel consumption and therefore cruising range. There may well also be some historical significance in the use of the 850-cc engine: many of Moto Guzzi's best-loved touring machines of the past were of this capacity, among them the T3 and the California of the 1970s.

Despite having a smaller engine, the 850 Norge loses little in luxuries compared with its bigger brother: standard equipment includes a manually height-adjustable windshield (as opposed to an electric one on the 1200), an anti-lock braking system, electric power points to run heated jackets and so on, and a pair of capacious, colour-matched panniers.

The chances are this 'baby' Norge will be put to greater all-round use than its slightly more unwieldy stablemate. One can imagine riding it to work Monday to Friday before taking off straight from the office for a long weekend of stress-busting touring.

Engine
877 cc, air-cooled, v-twin, eight-valve, four-stroke
Power
56 kW (75 bhp) @ 7800 rpm
Torque
70 Nm (52 ft lb) @ 6800 rpm
Gearbox
Six-speed
Final drive
Shaft
Weight
238 kg (525 lb) (est.)
Top speed
185 km/h (115 mph)

SUZUKI HAYABUSA LIMITED EDITION

While the aim of this book is to bring you each year the world's latest motorcycles, we felt it right to set aside these two pages for a machine that first arrived at the end of the last century. It was in 1999 that the Suzuki Hayabusa first scorched on to the pages of the motorcycle press by claiming the title of the 'world's fastest production motorcycle', thanks to its out-of-the-box ability to streak to an indicated 322 km/h (200 mph).

Since then faster-accelerating machines have come and gone, but no other has matched the legendary 'busa for sheer, outright speed – partly, of course, because of a subsequent agreement among manufacturers to limit their bikes to a top speed of 300 km/h (186 mph). Now, however, Suzuki has decided to kill off the bike, at least in its current form, and to mark the occasion the firm has produced a limited edition of 'grand finale' machines finished in special white-and-silver livery and fitted with a numbered plaque.

We suspect that more than a few will be bought for museums and small private collections. After all, a motorcycle that can truly claim to be the world's fastest doesn't come along every day.

Engine
1298 cc, liquid-cooled, double-overhead-camshaft, four-cylinder, four-stroke
Power
130 kW (175 bhp) @ 9800 rpm
Torque
140 Nm (103 ft lb) @ 7000 rpm
Gearbox
Six-speed
Final drive
Chain
Weight
215 kg (474 lb)
Top speed
312 km/h (194 mph)

SUZUKI
GSX 1300 R

VICTORY

VICTORY VISION TOUR AND STREET

Victory, the 'other' American motorcycle maker, looks set to offer a type of machine that its longer-established rival Harley-Davidson never has: a true touring bike with luxury refinements.

The Victory Tourer merges the traditional v-twin engine with the type of softer, curvier body styling more often seen on European and Japanese machines. It is available in two versions, Vision Street and Vision Tour, both aimed squarely at riders who want to travel rather than to cruise. The Tour, with its vast, armchair-style pillion seat, is a little more comfortable, but both models have enough tank capacity to cover at least 322 km (200 miles) between fuel stops.

The Tour also offers 110 litres (3.9 cu. ft) of storage in its integrated panniers. Its huge, wrap-around fairing with streamlined, built-in mirrors and over-the-top direction indicators make this a motorcycle that only the brave would consider using as day-to-day urban transport, despite a reasonably low, 67.3-cm (26.5-in.) seat height designed to assist with low-speed manoeuvrability – essential, given the 166.9-cm (65.7-in.) wheelbase.

A comprehensive options list means that buyers of either of the Victory tourer models may accessorize their machines to their personal specification with such extras as a stereo system, GPS navigation, heated grips and seats and anti-lock braking. The large expanses of bodywork also invite the type of eye-catching, one-off paint schemes that riders in the tourer/cruiser market often favour.

There is no doubt that Victory's largest creation to date takes the concept of the American v-twin to a new level, but whether it will be able to woo many of Harley-Davidson's large and famously loyal band of customers remains to be seen.

Engine
1634 cc, air- and oil-cooled, fuel-injected, single-overhead-camshaft, four-stroke
Power
63 kW (85 bhp) @ 5000 rpm
Torque
136 kW (100 ft lb) @ 3500 rpm
Gearbox
Six-speed overdrive
Final drive
Belt
Weight
305 kg (672 lb) (est.)
Top speed
185 km/h (115 mph)

STREET, NAKED AND MUSCLE

SUZUKI

MANA850

APRILIA 850 MANA

Recently Aprilia has really gone into overdrive with its model range, and not only do the bikes look good and perform well, but they are now also beginning to break new technological ground. The Mana, unveiled at the 2006 EICMA show in Milan, is just the first of what we believe will be a new breed of large-capacity motorcycle – the 'twist and go' all-rounder.

This wiry-looking naked features an innovative, computer-controlled automatic transmission that can be used in one of three modes for touring, sports or wet-weather applications, or switched to manual operation for a more traditional feel, with the seven ratios being shifted either by handlebar-mounted push buttons or a conventional foot lever.

Handling promises to be excellent, because of both the Mana's light weight and a stiff, trellis frame that is supported by 43-mm (1.7-in.) inverted forks and a one-piece aluminium swing arm. Radial-mounted brake calipers do the stopping, and an underseat fuel cell ensures both a low centre of gravity and some extra storage space inside the dummy tank.

This motorcycle goes some way towards melding the practicality of a maxi scooter with the looks, handling, performance and street cred of a 'real' motorcycle, and it deserves to be a hit.

Incidentally, it is interesting that it is a relatively small Italian manufacturer that has instigated the use of automatic transmission on a full-sized motorcycle. We suspect that the Japanese will be following Aprilia's example very soon.

Engine
839 cc, liquid-cooled, fuel-injected, v-twin, four-stroke
Power
56 kW (75 bhp) @ 7250 rpm
Torque
77 Nm (57 ft lb) @ 8000 rpm
Gearbox
Seven-speed switchable automatic
Final drive
Chain
Weight
185 kg (408 lb) (est.)
Top speed
193 km/h (120 mph)

APRILIA SL 750 SHIVER

The first time we saw the name 'Shiver' used by Aprilia was back in 1998, when it was applied to a rather ugly prototype that never came to fruition. The looks of this twenty-first-century Shiver more than make up for past mistakes, however, particularly in the case of the gold-frame versions, which are really eye-catching. Neat styling touches abound, from the unusual headlamp to the chunky, triangular exhaust tailpipes, which are echoed in the small, similarly shaped direction indicators.

The Shiver is intended to steal some sales from the much-loved but decidedly long-in-the-tooth Ducati Monster, and uses a fuel-injected, liquid-cooled 750-cc engine rather than a litre-plus one. Aprilia claims that this ultra-compact powerplant provides traditionally impressive v-twin torque with similar peak power to a four-cylinder engine of the same capacity, thanks to the use of cylinder heads that are equipped with twin spark plugs. The unit is certainly far superior to the Monster's air-cooled motors and should be both cheaper and easier to maintain, too, because of the use of chain-drive camshafts rather than the sometimes troublesome belt system used by Ducati.

Like the Mana (see pp. 128–29), the Shiver has a trellis frame in which aluminium and steel are mixed to create a relatively inexpensive combination of lightness and rigidity. With inverted front forks and a one-piece swing arm suspended by a single shock absorber, the machine promises sharp and nimble handling, while race-style, radially mounted brake calipers ensure that it stops as well as it goes.

Engine
750 cc, double-overhead-camshaft, three-cylinder, four-stroke
Power
71 kW (95 bhp) @ 9000 rpm
Torque
78 kW (105 ft lb) @ 7000 rpm
Gearbox
Six-speed
Final drive
Chain
Weight
189 kg (417 lb)
Top speed
201 km/h (125 mph)

Benelli

BENELLI DUE 756

Divide 1130 by three and multiply the result by two, and what do you get? Well, 753.3, to be precise, but that number does go some way to explaining why Benelli's fabulous-looking new twin is called the Due 756. The full explanation is that its liquid-cooled, parallel-twin engine has been created by lopping off one of the cylinders from the motor used in the Tornado and Tre-K 1130 models.

The decision not to create an all-new powerplant could have been a question of economy, or it could simply have been that Benelli saw that the excellent 1130 engine design had not been exploited to the full. Either way, its appearance shows that the large-capacity parallel twin is returning to favour after a long period in the doldrums. Triumph's Bonneville range and Kawasaki's Versys both use this classic configuration, and it is one to which riders raised on v-twins and in-line fours are gradually warming.

Although parallel-twin units instantly recall British motorcycles of the 1950s and onwards, there is nothing old-fashioned about the Due 756, particularly in the aesthetics department. Even before the bike went into production the design won the 'open' category of the 2006 Motorcycle Design Awards, thanks to the radical treatment of everything from its stacked headlamp unit to the triangulated, short exhaust pipe. Here it is included among the naked bikes because that is where it seems to belong, but from certain angles it could equally easily deserve the description 'supermoto', and the use of inverted forks, radial brakes and a lightweight frame certainly make it race-able. But what's in a name? This is a fabulous-looking machine and that is all that matters.

Engine
756 cc, liquid-cooled, double-overhead-camshaft, parallel-twin, four-stroke
Power
60 kW (80 bhp) @ 9000 rpm (est.)
Torque
N/A
Gearbox
Six-speed
Final drive
Chain
Weight
N/A
Top speed
193 km/h (120 mph) (est.)

BMW HP2 MEGAMOTO

Engine
1170 cc, air- and oil-cooled, flat-twin, four-stroke
Power
82 kW (110 bhp) @ 7500 rpm
Torque
120 Nm (88 ft lb) @ 6000 rpm
Gearbox
Six-speed
Final drive
Shaft
Weight
178 kg (392 lb)
Top speed
193 km/h (120 mph) plus

BMW caused jaws to drop when it unveiled its awesome HP2 enduro machine in 2005. It was large, it was fast, it was expensive, and it has proved surprisingly capable in off-road competition. Not long after its launch, however, it became apparent that there were plenty of road riders who would buy an HP2 to use on tarmac, and so BMW responded with an optional set of 'supermoto' wheels fitted with sticky tyres.

In turn, those optional wheels led to the creation of the Megamoto version shown here – a production HP2 that has been adapted for pure street or track use. The first significant change can be seen in the cast-alloy wheels, fat road tyres and a lowered suspension that comprises fully adjustable, inverted front forks and a top-quality Ohlins rear shock absorber. All of these combine to make the bike handle remarkably well on twisting smaller roads.

BMW has also boosted the HP2's already impressive torque and power outputs to provide additional punch coming out of corners and better high-speed capability, all of which is backed up by the addition of an extra front brake disc over the single-disc set-up of the original machine. In terms of braking, the Megamoto is now claimed to compare favourably with any road-going sports bike – quite something for what is still an off-road-based hybrid.

The Megamoto also gets a few frills that are missing from the HP2, such as a tachometer, a more powerful headlight and a lower seat to make it easier to handle in traffic. Its 'premium-product' status (remember that this is an expensive, hand-built, limited-production machine) is further evident in the use of carbon fibre for the fuel-tank cover and bikini fairing, while a first-rate Akrapovic exhaust system gives the Megamoto a bark of which to be proud, as well as improving torque and throttle response.

BMW
HP2

BUELL XB12 STT

Buell's stock list is already full to bursting with naked street bikes, but the XB12 STT is a little different from all the others because it is based on the Ulysses 'adventure-sports' model and is therefore more of a road-biased trail bike with a touch of supermoto thrown in. It has long-travel suspension, a solo seat unit, wide, cross-braced handlebars and American-style flat-track racing-number boards at the front and sides.

But the other part of this bike's three-way split personality makes it capable of knee-down cornering angles, impeccable handling on secondary roads and even long-distance touring – provided, of course, you can tolerate the rather harsh ride that results from the extremely short wheelbase that is a Buell trademark. This, combined with a steep steering angle and firm suspension, allows the XB12 STT to change direction more rapidly and with greater finesse than many an all-out sports bike – a trait that has been central to the design of the firm's machines since the beginning.

In addition, the STT gets all the other Buell signature touches, including the underslung exhaust system, rim-mounted front brake disc, belt drive and underseat fuel storage to keep the centre of gravity as low as possible – another factor that contributes to its excellent handling. Laden with torque, agile, versatile and fast, this could be the ultimate motorcycle for some riders. Others, though, will find it essentially unrefined, harsh and difficult to live with. But it is for this second group that the Japanese make motorcycles.

Engine
1203 cc, air-cooled, overhead-valve, v-twin, four-stroke
Power
77 kW (103 bhp) @ 6800 rpm
Torque
114 Nm (84 ft lb) @ 6000 rpm
Gearbox
Five-speed
Final drive
Belt
Weight
181 kg (399 lb)
Top speed
217 km/h (135 mph) (est.)

CONFEDERATE HELLCAT 20LTD

Engine
1853cc , air-cooled, single-overhead-camshaft, v-twin
Power
108 kW (145 bhp) @ 6000 rpm (est.)
Torque
214 Nm (158 ft lb) @ 4500 rpm (est.)
Gearbox
Five-speed
Final drive
Chain
Weight
231 kg (510 lb)
Top speed
N/A

If proof were needed that motorcycles are now truly established as a luxury item, this is it: a limited-edition Confederate Hellcat that has been produced specifically to be sold via the internet on a new, luxury-goods 'e-tail' site called 20ltd.

The site, which is published in five languages, is the world's first electronic shop offering strictly limited-edition goods, ranging from the finest shoes to the best watches and from private jets to far-out motorcycles. The crux of 20ltd is that no item will be available in an edition of greater than twenty examples, and in order to comply with this criterion, Confederate had to produce this special version of its F113 Hellcat, which boasts even more power and torque than the already raunchy standard machine.

That means you get 108 kW (145 bhp) at the rear wheel instead of 98 kW (132 bhp) and 214 Nm (158 ft lb) of torque instead of 204 Nm (150 ft lb). It is unlikely, though, that the wealthy buyer of the limited edition will notice the difference. He or she will still be catapulted down the road to the accompaniment of a cacophonous exhaust bark (which is emitted through the swing arm), only to find him- or herself, within 2.8 seconds, travelling at 1.6 km (1 mile) per minute.

The buyer will also join an exclusive Confederate owners club that includes Hollywood stars Tom Cruise and Brad Pitt and rock star Bruce Springsteen. But do they actually ride their bikes, one wonders?

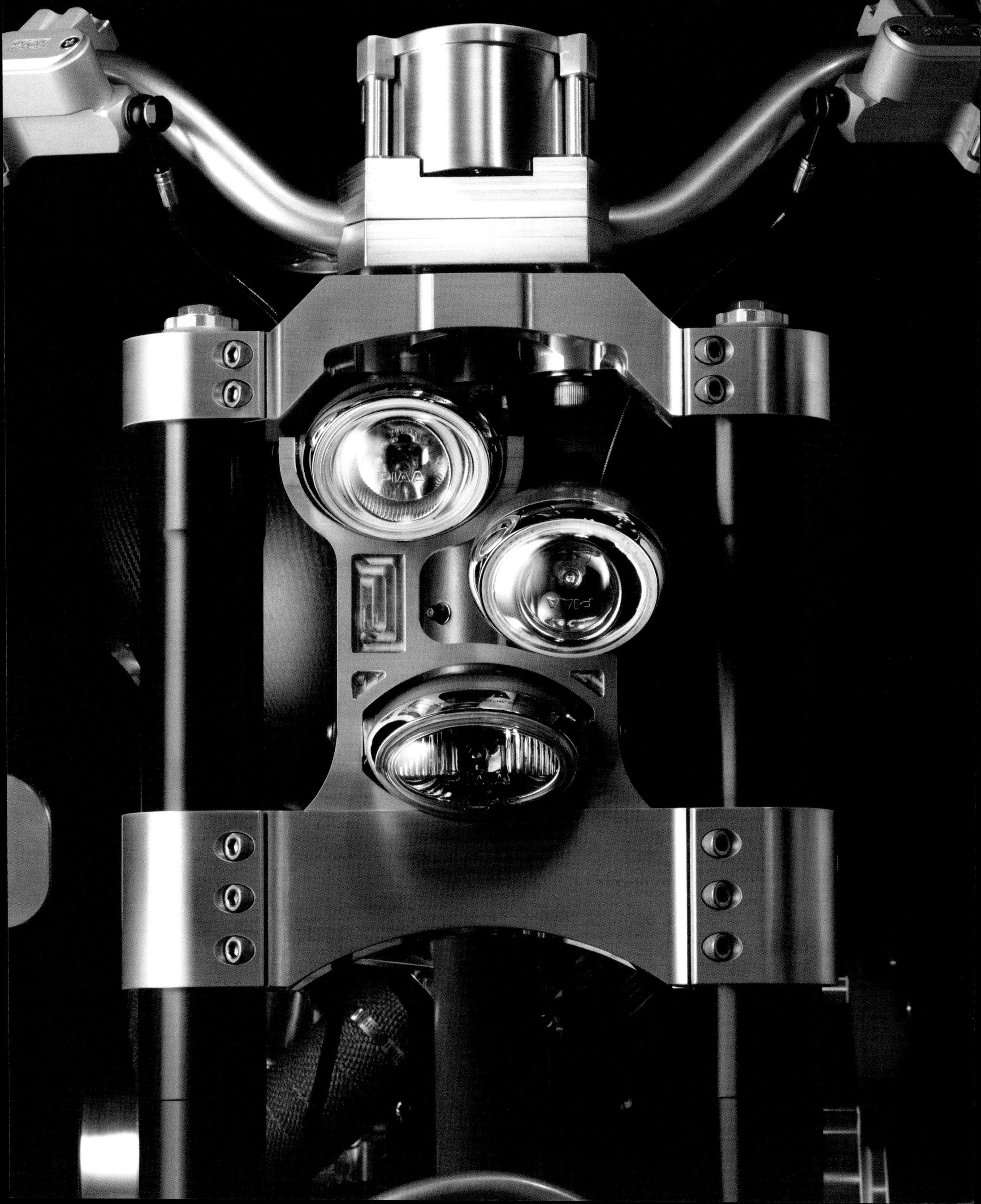
PIAA

MULHACÉN
125
DERBI

MULHACÉN
125
DERBI

DERBI MULHACÉN 125

When we introduced the Derbi Mulhacén 659 in the first edition of *The New Motorcycle Yearbook*, it was no more than a much-anticipated prototype. The larger-engined version is now in production, and the range has been expanded with this 125-cc addition.

With all things retro still regarded as extremely cool, this learner-capacity machine should be well received by the seventeen-to-twenty-five age group. Its cobby appearance gives it a purposeful personality and, despite having an overall 1960s look, it abounds with touches that ensure it is entirely contemporary: from the flat silver paint scheme to the jet-black wheel rims, and from the softly triangulated headlamp to the electronic instrument panel. Note, too, the delicate webs that have been created within the front and rear brake discs; they are minor works of art.

Although the Mulhacén 125 is aimed first and foremost at the young market, its use as a deft commuter bike for more mature riders should not be underestimated. The 125-cc, twin-cam engine is extremely punchy, and the wide handlebars and tight turning circle make this an ideal machine for the cut and thrust of urban travel.

Engine
123 cc, liquid-cooled, double-overhead-camshaft, single-cylinder, four-stroke
Power
11 kW (15 bhp) @ 8500 rpm (est.)
Torque
14 Nm (10 ft lb) @ 7700 rpm (est.)
Gearbox
Six-speed
Final drive
Chain
Weight
130 kg (287 lb) (est.)
Top speed
113 km/h (70 mph)

DUCATI MONSTER S4R TESTASTRETTA

Engine
998 cc, overhead-camshaft, l-twin, eight-valve, four-stroke
Power
97 kW (130 bhp) @ 9500 rpm
Torque
104 Nm (77 ft lb) @ 7500 rpm
Gearbox
Six-speed
Final drive
Chain
Weight
177 kg (390 lb)
Top speed
241 km/h (150 mph)

Ducati's best-selling Monster has been around since 1993, and there have been more than thirty different variations on the theme, the latest of which is the S4R Testastretta, one of the most powerful and best-handling big-bore Monsters ever made. The 'Testastretta' of the name means that this bike has the 'narrow-head' engine used in the 999 sports bike, which punches out a dramatic 97 kW (130 bhp) at the rear wheel.

The bike differs from the previously launched S4Rs – the top-of-the-range Monster – in having new, inverted Showa front forks and rear suspension that is different from the better-specification Ohlins equipment fitted to the S. Nevertheless, it is said by Ducati to fulfil 'a very important role' in the brand's latest line-up.

In truth, though, it is barely different from the S – just a little less expensive. And this makes one wonder how much longer the Monster line can remain viable before a serious revamp proves vital in the face of the ever more radical naked machines being produced by the opposition. Simply 'mixing and matching' a few components and claiming to have produced a new model does not really cut the mustard nowadays, yet who could blame a brand with an all-time classic on its hands for milking it for all its worth?

There is not much more to say about the S4R Testastretta other than that, as Ducati puts it, the bike has 'a prettier look thanks to the new fork bottom end' and 'is now available in two new colour schemes: titanium with a black stripe and red with a white stripe'.

DUCATI

DUCATI

HARLEY-DAVIDSON

HARLEY-DAVIDSON XR1200

With the marque's long-standing reputation as a maker of chrome-clad cruisers, it might come as news to learn that Harley-Davidson is also the producer of the most successful racing motorcycle of all time, bar none. The XR750 is a legend in the world of flat-track competition, having taken no fewer than twenty-six championship titles since its introduction in 1970.

With hindsight, it is surprising that Harley-Davidson has waited until now to take advantage of this remarkable sporting heritage to produce a road-going version of the XR. A few years ago it introduced a Sportster-based model named the XL883R that paid homage to the race bike in terms of its paint scheme rather than by emulating its performance or handling. The all-new XR1200, though, is far closer to the real thing.

Unveiled at the end of 2006 as a prototype model, the bike attracted such a positive reaction that the company quickly decided to put it into production. Aimed mainly at the European market, it is said to have the most powerful version of the venerable air-cooled, v-twin engine ever to be made available on a standard model. This was made possible by the application of a few internal tweaks and, most significantly, the use of fuel injection and an electronically controlled 'active air intake' system.

The handling and brakes have been considerably upgraded to cope with the extra power, too. The Showa front forks are of the inverted type found on all state-of-the-art sports bikes, and the triple, drilled brake discs are teamed with Nissin racing calipers and cast wheels that reduce unsprung weight. Unusually for a Harley, this bike is also capable of quite extreme lean angles, thanks to the fact that the footrests and controls have been placed much further back than on the cruiser bikes. It is fitted with special Dunlop Qualifier tyres.

The twin, stacked exhaust system is a much tamer, street-legal version of the barking, straight-through affair worn by the race bikes, and the XR1200 also gets a neat pillion seat. The competition look is picked up in the short front mudguard, flat-track-style handlebars and, of course, the orange, black and white paint scheme that makes the XR750 so recognizable, although other colours will be available.

The XR1200 is being billed as Harley-Davidson's first real sports bike and, although it has been a long time coming, it deserves to do well. And no doubt we'll see, and hear, plenty of after-market customized versions that come even closer in looks and performance to the legendary 750.

Engine
1199 cc, air-cooled, v-twin, four-stroke
Power
67 kW (90 bhp) @ 6250 rpm (est.)
Torque
95 Nm (70 ft lb) @ 4000 rpm (est.)
Gearbox
Five-speed
Final drive
Belt
Weight
159 kg (350 lb) (est.)
Top speed
193 km/h (120 mph) (est.)

HARTFORD HD200

Engine
197 cc, overhead-camshaft, single-cylinder, four-stroke
Power
11 kW (15 bhp) @ 7000 rpm (est.)
Torque
15 Nm (11 ft lb) @ 4000 rpm (est.)
Gearbox
Five-speed
Final drive
Chain
Weight
130 kg (287 lb)
Top speed
113 km/h (70 mph)

There was a time when buyers were spoiled for choice in the 200-cc class: Honda, Yamaha and Kawasaki all built machines of this capacity and sold them around the world as bread-and-butter commuter bikes. Nowadays the category is far less popular, but the Taiwanese brand Hartford is doing its bit to revive it with the no-frills HD200. The marque is little known in Europe, but Hartford has been building motorcycles for more than forty years under the overall control of a well-established Japanese manufacturer – Honda.

This helps a great deal with quality control and ensures that Hartford machines are all based on tried-and-trusted designs. The engines, for example, are principally developed from the ubiquitous CG125, with the necessary upgrades to ensure that they meet modern emissions standards. But in fact the HD200 has an engine all of its own, a new powerplant that has been designed and built specifically for it.

The additional 75 cc of capacity over that of a 125 might not sound like much, but it makes the machine disproportionately more responsive and enjoyable to ride, whether as an in-town commuter bike – which it is primarily intended to be – or for occasional forays on to major roads. The wide handlebars and low seat height help with manoeuvrability, and a fat rear tyre puts plenty of rubber on the road for assured handling.

In terms of cycle parts, however, the Hartford is very much a machine from the bargain basement. A basic disc brake at the front is paired with a rear drum, twin shock absorbers of a thirty-year-old design support the back end, and the mudguards are made from lightly chromed steel that, at a guess, will start showing its quality after a single British winter.

For a budget commuting machine that looks like a 'real' motorcycle, however, and performs far better than the average 125-cc commuter, Hartford's little wonder really takes some beating.

km/h

PASS
LIGHTS
OFF
HORN

HONDA CB600F HORNET

Honda launched the original Hornet in 1998, and it was a darned good idea. The combination of street-bike looks, an engine from the CBR 600 sports bike, an affordable price and Honda's legendary reliability proved an instant hit, and the Hornet became the default choice of all kinds of riders, from newly qualified novices to couriers and middle-aged commuters.

Since then the model has been upgraded three or four times, but never so radically as now. The new Hornet has a slightly detuned version of the very latest engine fitted to the current CBR 600RR sports bike and a chassis and suspension set-up that makes it handle like a dream. The result is power to match some 750-cc rivals, giving sports-bike performance in a package suitable for everyday use.

The all-new frame and swing-arm combination is forged from aluminium to keep weight to a minimum. The five-spoke alloy wheels are also made of aluminium, making the Hornet the lightest machine in its class.

Nods to practicality include an enlarged fuel tank and a visually pleasing exhaust system fitted with a short, race-style silencer that is far more appropriate for carrying luggage and a passenger than the previous high-mounted, underseat version. The small, hawk-like fairing nacelle is said to have been modelled on a medieval knight's helmet – why, only Honda knows – and is there more for aesthetic reasons than to reduce wind blast, which is a shame, as this is possibly the quickest naked in the 600-cc class.

Practical, fast, fun, good-looking and fine-handling, the Hornet looks set to sting the opposition once again.

Engine
599 cc, liquid-cooled, double-overhead-camshaft, four-cylinder, four-stroke
Power
76 kW (102 bhp) @ 12,000 rpm
Torque
64 Nm (47 ft lb) @ 10,500 rpm
Gearbox
Six-speed
Final drive
Chain
Weight
173 kg (381 lb)
Top speed
233 km/h (145 mph)

HYOSUNG GT650X

South Korean bike builder Hyosung is making significant inroads into Europe with its range of well-engineered, budget-priced motorcycles that are designed to compete in some of the hardest-fought sectors of the market. For example, in the middleweight category its GT650R goes head to head with Japan and Europe's best, and now it is about to launch a naked bike based on similar mechanicals that will challenge such favourites as Suzuki's SV650, Kawasaki's ER-6N and the Ducati Monster.

Unveiled as a prototype at the 2006 UK Motorcycle Show, the GT650X showed potential to match the best of the opposition in terms of looks, with its lean, mean, angular appearance and some touches cheekily stolen from other manufacturers' existing machines. Check out that stubby, side-exit exhaust pipe, for example. Doesn't it recall Yamaha's R6 sports bike? And isn't the trellis frame more than a little Monster-like? And remember the Cagiva Raptor's similarly styled cockpit fairing?

One area in which the Hyosung doesn't imitate its rivals, however, is price. This bike is expected to sell for less than £4000 in the United Kingdom, making it a lot cheaper than anything similar from the better-known brands. So long as Hyosung ensures that the cost is not reflected in the machine's reliability or the longevity of its finish, it will continue to win customers.

The brand has already established a strong following, and its GT650R sports machine is selling well to both road riders and those looking for an affordable machine from which to strip such superfluous components as lights and indicators, for track use.

Engine
647 cc, liquid-cooled, double-overhead-camshaft, v-twin, four-stroke
Power
60 kW (80 bhp) @ 9000 rpm
Torque
61 Nm (45 ft lb) @ 7500 rpm
Gearbox
Six-speed
Final drive
Chain
Weight
200 kg (441 lb)
Top speed
193 km/h (120 mph)

HYOSUNG

Kawasaki
Kawasaki
Kawasaki
Kawasaki

KAWASAKI VERSYS

Japanese motorcycle manufacturers have an ability to watch what the opposition is doing, leave a period of grace, and then do the same thing – only better. This might well be the case with the Versys, which seems to have been spawned from the thinking behind the Multistrada 'motorcycle for all roads' launched by Ducati in 2003.

Like the Multistrada, the Versys has a hint of trail-bike styling about it, but it is not really intended for off-road use. Instead, it combines the comfortable, upright riding position and ample leg room of a trail bike with a punchy road-biased engine and lovely, taut handling. The Ducati does exactly the same things, and does them well, but the Versys is far less expensive, considerably more attractive, and probably less fragile mechanically.

Although it feels and looks sharp and fresh, the heart of this motorcycle is its parallel-twin engine, which is based on a design that Kawasaki has been using for years, but clever tuning has made it powerful where it counts, fuel-efficient and, above all, fun.

Kawasaki has ensured that the Versys seems very modern by giving it a similar subframe to its sister machine, the ER-6, an unusually shaped headlight and an underslung exhaust system along the lines of those pioneered on Buell machines.

To enhance the touring abilities of the Versys, the small screen is height adjustable, the fuel tank has a useful 19-litre (4.2-gallon) capacity – sufficient for almost 400 km (250 miles) of gentle riding – and a range of custom-made luggage is available. Anti-lock brakes are also offered as an option.

Engine
650 cc, liquid-cooled, fuel-injected, parallel-twin, four-stroke
Power
48 kW (64 bhp) @ 8000 rpm
Torque
61 Nm (45 ft lb) @ 6800 rpm
Gearbox
Six-speed
Final drive
Chain
Weight
181 kg (399 lb)
Top speed
193 km/h (120 mph)

KAWASAKI Z750

Engine
748 cc, liquid-cooled, double-overhead-camshaft, four-cylinder, four-stroke
Power
79 kW (106 bhp) @ 10,500 rpm
Torque
78 Nm (57 ft lb) @ 7300 rpm
Gearbox
Six-speed
Final drive
Chain
Weight
203 kg (448 lb)
Top speed
225 km/h (140 mph)

The outgoing Z750 was a no-frills, budget four-cylinder machine that was often criticized for having bland looks and bland performance. True, it was built down to a price and, yes, it was based on the kind of engineering that would not have seemed particularly cutting-edge even twenty years ago. But, as a reliable, easy-to-live-with motorcycle for all-round use, it was actually pretty good. The usefulness remains with the new Z750, but no one could accuse it of looking bland. Mean, aggressive and attacking, but never bland. From the massive, slab-sided steel frame to the equally massive triangular-section silencer, this looks like a motorcycle that shouldn't be trifled with. It has the heart to live up to its promise, too.

Punching out 79 kW (106 bhp), the high-revving engine has enough go to push the relatively light Z750 to around 225 km/h (140 mph), and since Kawasaki's engineers have adopted the principle of mass centralization used heavily in the design of pure sports bikes, handling is also deliciously crisp.

Petal-edged brake discs are fitted for enhanced cooling and wet-weather performance (although the calipers are still of the old side-mounting type rather than being a modern radial-fit), and the instrument panel – comprising a dominant rev counter and a smaller digital speedometer – blends nicely with the threatening-looking headlamp cowling.

Z750

Kawasaki

Kawasaki

KAWASAKI Z1000

The arrival of Kawasaki's Z series of machines during the early 1970s signalled a sea change in motorcycling: Honda had already invented the 'superbike' with its four-cylinder CB750 in 1969, but four years later Kawasaki took things a stage further with its 900-cc Z1, which, at the time, was the most powerful production motorcycle ever made.

The big K still upholds its long-standing reputation for building powerhouse machines, and its latest supersports bikes, such as the ZX10 and the ZX6R, are no exception. But the original sit-up-and-beg Z models are still remembered with rose-tinted affection by many motorcyclists of a certain age, and these are the people to whom Kawasaki hopes to cater with the latest Z1000.

This is a heavily reworked version of a bike launched in 2003 as a modern take on the 1970s Z1000, which itself evolved from the original Z1. The 2003 model used important styling cues from the early machine, notably the four-into-four exhaust system with two stacked silencers on either side – a feature that all lovers of classic Kawasakis expect to be present on restored examples. But somehow the look didn't translate, and the modern Z seemed to lack the sheer presence that the early bikes possessed in spades. It seemed strangely small and just too refined.

The latest Z1000 certainly looks beefier, and the exhaust-pipe heritage has been given a neat twist in the form of a pair of massive, siamesed silencers that allow the engine to breathe better and, along with various camshaft and valve modifications, provide a worthwhile improvement in low and mid-range torque for better roll-on performance.

Brakes and suspension, too, have been upgraded, and the frame has not only been stretched slightly but has also been made more flexible. This is quite ironic, since one of the main criticisms of the 1970s Z1 was that the chassis was too 'bendy' for the power of the engine.

Such modern accoutrements as radially mounted brake calipers and petal-edged brake discs are also light years ahead of those fitted to the original, and features including fuel injection, electronic instrumentation and aerodynamic bikini fairing make this very much a Z of the twenty-first century. But, given the choice between this one and the original, I confess I'm just old-fashioned.

Engine
953 cc, liquid-cooled, double-overhead-camshaft, four-cylinder, four-stroke
Power
93 kW (125 bhp) @ 10,000 rpm
Torque
99 Nm (73 ft lb) @ 8200 rpm
Gearbox
Six-speed
Final drive
Chain
Weight
198 kg (437 lb)
Top speed
233 km/h (145 mph)

MOTO GUZZI GRISO 8V

Engine
1151 cc, air-cooled, overhead-camshaft, v-twin, eight-valve, four-stroke
Power
82 kW (110 bhp) @ 9500 rpm
Torque
109 Nm (80 ft lb) @ 6500 rpm
Gearbox
Six-speed
Final drive
Shaft
Weight
230 kg (507 lb) (est.)
Top speed
225 km/h (140 mph) (est.)

Moto Guzzi's aggressively styled Griso met with wide approval when it was launched in 2005, marking for many the moment when the formerly glorious brand put itself well and truly back on the map after a line of rather mediocre machines that failed to live up to past successes, such as the Le Mans I, the 850T3 and the racy 750S of the early 1970s.

Moto Guzzi called the original Griso 1100 a 'techno-custom', which implied that it was intended for relaxed, laid-back riding and provided a good excuse to fit it with a relatively uninspiring, old-fashioned engine that is based on the agricultural unit originally conceived for the V7 more than forty years ago. It must be said, though, that despite being somewhat outdated, this engine remains surprisingly potent and exciting.

Once the Griso hit the streets, however, it quickly became clear that owners wanted a bike that performed not just as well as it looked, but even better – and Moto Guzzi has responded with this, the 8V version. Using a highly modified, 1200-cc version of the classic v-twin engine with four valves per cylinder (hence 8V), the Griso now has a heady output of 82 kW (110 bhp), which makes for highly respectable acceleration and a top speed of around 225 km/h (140 mph).

To emphasize the machine's sportier nature, the ergonomic arrangement of the footrests, seat and handlebars has been altered to provide a more racy riding position, and the bodywork side panels have been smoothed and streamlined. Brembo radial brakes take care of stopping the bike, which is fitted with top-quality, nitride-coated front forks and massive, 320-mm (12.6-in.) wave-edge brake discs. And look at that wonderful siamesed exhaust – surely one of the best-looking systems ever used on a twin-cylinder motorcycle.

Despite its new, high-speed capabilities, however, the naked Griso is still a practical machine, partly thanks to its inherently long wheelbase, a typical Moto Guzzi trait, which not only makes it comfortable for the rider, but also provides plenty of pillion space.

MOTO GUZZI 1200 SPORT

The Moto Guzzi 1200 Sport is one of the coolest and meanest-looking production motorcycles to be released for some time. From the rear-set footrests to the race-style number boards, and from the wave-edge brake discs to the low-rise handlebars, this is one of those machines that just seems right from all angles.

Despite its 'Sport' tag, Guzzi's aggressive-looking 1200 also lends itself to long-distance touring, thanks to its lazy yet powerful engine, tall gearing, comfortable seating for two, that surprisingly effective mini fairing and the extensive range of luggage that has been custom-made for it. But most riders will use the 1200 Sport as a highly competent all-rounder in the best tradition of motorcycling.

The bike's shaft drive makes it practical, its riding position makes it easy to handle in traffic, and its turn of speed and handling make it fun, so what more could one ask? How about a race kit? Guzzi has thought of that, too, and for a little extra cash owners can soup up their Sport with a pair of hand-polished air ducts that replace the standard air-filter box, a straight-through race exhaust system and a re-mapped ECU that makes the bike's already punchy power delivery even more exciting.

As a highly versatile naked, this machine really takes some beating. Let's just hope that, under the ownership of Piaggio, Moto Guzzi's former reliability problems (mainly stemming from electrical issues) will stay just where they are – in the past.

Engine
1151 cc, overhead-camshaft, v-twin, two-valve, four-stroke
Power
71 kW (95 bhp) @ 7800 rpm
Torque
100 Nm (74 ft lb) @ 5800 rpm
Gearbox
Six-speed
Final drive
Shaft
Weight
229 kg (505 lb)
Top speed
225 km/h (140 mph)

MOTO MORINI 1200 CORSARO VELOCE

Engine
1187 cc
Power
104 kW (140 bhp) @ 8500 rpm
Torque
123 Nm (91 ft lb) @ 6500 rpm
Gearbox
Six-speed
Final drive
Chain
Weight
196 kg (432 lb)
Top speed
225 km/h (140 mph)

If you want a big-bore, four-cylinder naked, go Japanese; if you want a big-bore, v-twin naked, go Italian. With its low-down power qualities, the v-twin format lends itself well to naked motorcycles because they are all about fast, corner-to-corner squirting and around-town manoeuvrability, rather than sustained motorway cruising.

But that's not to say the Corsaro Veloce lacks the guts for high-speed riding. With an arm-wrenching 104 kW (140 bhp) on tap, this lunatic machine will keep on going for as long as the rider can hang on in the wind blast. The 'Veloce' of this model's name indicates that it is the souped-up version of the standard Corsaro, which means an extra 11 kW (15 bhp) from an upgraded engine-management chip, free-breathing, just-legal exhaust pipes and sportier, rear-set footrests.

The compact, short-stroke engine is a fast-revving unit that provides peak torque at around 6500 rpm, 2000 revs short of the red line. Make the most of that torque and you will find yourself leaning over the handlebars trying to keep the front wheel on the ground and rejoicing in the Corsaro's incredible stomp. Italian bikes are famously good handlers, and this one is no exception. Its short-chassis configuration is somewhat reminiscent of a Buell streetfighter and makes bend-swinging a delight, particularly since it is to the accompaniment of those growling sports exhausts.

Typically, cycle parts are top-of-the-range, with brakes by Brembo, forks by Marzocchi and rear suspension by Sachs. This is the type of motorcycle that 'lads' mags' will sum up with one word: 'mental'.

CORSARO

CORSARO
PIRELLI

SHELBY
RUCKER PERFORMANCE

SHELBY
RUCKER PERFORMANCE

SHELBY

Carroll Shelby is a living legend in the world of American sports cars. A successful racing driver during the 1950s, he broke land-speed records at Bonneville in 1954 and won the Le Mans 24 Hours in 1959 with team-mate Roy Salvadori, before giving up racing in 1960 and turning his hand to automotive design.

Shelby's first and greatest achievement in the field was to shoe-horn a large-capacity V8 engine into the British-built AC sports car. The result was the Shelby Cobra, one of the fastest and most talked-about road cars ever created, and it lead to an agreement with Ford to build extra powerful versions of its highly successful Mustang coupé.

The Shelby Mustang helped make Shelby a household name, but it is only now, at the age of eighty-four, that he has decided to turn his hand to motorcycle production with the simply named Shelby, a bike that perpetuates the American theory that 'ya can't beat cubes'. That's cubic inches, for all you Europeans, and the Shelby has 128 of them, the equivalent of 2097 cc.

The long, low Shelby was developed in collaboration with custom-bike builder Rucker Performance and has a lightweight chassis with fully adjustable, inverted front forks, an air-damped rear shock absorber, carbon-fibre wheels and bodywork, and ceramic brake discs. The gearbox takes a cue from the world of drag racing by using compressed air to make high-speed shifts, although buyers can ask for almost any specification they want throughout the machine, provided they are willing to pay for the privilege.

Californian Bill Rucker, the founder of Rucker Performance, is famous for building spectacular motorcycles and claims that the Shelby is the 'ultimate' in American high-performance machines, thanks to the use of an all-new engine, designed and built by the performance house S & S, that churns out 119 kW (160 bhp). No more than twenty-five bikes are expected to be built each year.

Engine
2097 cc, fuel-injected, v-twin, four-stroke
Power
119 kW (160 bhp) @ 9000 rpm (est.)
Torque
N/A
Gearbox
Six-speed, air-shifter
Final drive
Chain
Weight
249 kg (550 lb)
Top speed
Up to 282 km/h (175 mph), depending on gearing

SUZUKI B-KING

Engine
1299 cc, liquid-cooled, fuel-injected, double-overhead-camshaft, four-cylinder, four-stroke
Power
N/A
Torque
N/A
Gearbox
Six-speed
Final drive
Chain
Weight
N/A
Top speed
241 km/h (150 mph) (est.)

Not many motorcycles are hailed as legendary before their launch, but the B-King certainly was. In fact, it took such a long time coming that many people wondered whether it could be a myth.

Originally unveiled as a radical concept machine at the Tokyo Motor Show in 2001, the B-King was so far out that nobody believed it would ever make the production stage; and most thought that if it did, the bike that eventually reached the streets would be a much tamer, toned-down version of the original design.

But Suzuki has surprised us all by closely maintaining the look and spirit of the early machine, even down to one of its best-loved 'signature' features: those almost cartoon-like underseat exhaust pipes, which wouldn't look out of place at the back of a jet fighter. Yet, even after unveiling the bike itself, Suzuki insisted on keeping its specifications a closely guarded secret, and it is still doing so as this edition of *The New Motorcycle Yearbook* goes to press.

However, the company did afford journalists a tantalizing glimpse of the B-King in action when it suddenly began circling Australia's Philip Island race circuit unannounced during the launch of the latest GSX-R 1000 sports bike. It is safe to assume that the engine is a version of the 1300-cc, four-cylinder unit that powers the legendary, soon-to-be-axed Hayabusa to a maximum speed of 322 km/h (200 mph). The frame is of massive, yet lightweight construction, and ancillary components, such as the radially mounted brake calipers, are all state of the art.

SUZUKI

SUZUKI

SUZUKI GSF 650N BANDIT/GSF G50S BANDIT

Suzuki's middleweight Bandit first appeared in the early 1990s and, after more than fifteen years in production with no major modifications, it was long overdue an overhaul. The result of that process is an all-new Bandit that, like its larger-engined brother, gets a water-cooled engine and many other improvements.

With considerably more torque and power available, the baby Bandit also needed a new chassis to keep everything travelling in the same direction. It has been given a very rigid yet very light aluminium-and-steel frame that is extremely compact, owing largely to the extraordinary efforts Suzuki's engineers have made to ensure that the engine of this high-revving middleweight is of pocket-sized proportions.

With narrow cylinder heads, a compact combustion chamber made possible by steep valve angles, a vertically stacked transmission and a small, high-output alternator, the powerplant is a good 25 per cent smaller than that fitted to the old model. The internals, too, are far advanced, many parts being treated with PVD (physical vapour deposition), which, by reducing friction, keeps wear to a minimum and performance to a maximum.

A practical stainless-steel exhaust system is fitted with an oxygen sensor linked to the engine management system to ensure efficient combustion in all conditions, while rider comforts include adjustable controls and an attractive LED instrument panel. Anti-lock brakes are available as an optional extra.

Engine
656 cc, liquid-cooled, fuel-injected, double-overhead-camshaft, four-cylinder, four-stroke
Power
N/A
Torque
N/A
Gearbox
Six-speed
Final drive
Chain
Weight
GSF 650N, 215 kg (474 lb) (ABS version 219 kg/483 lb); GSF 650S, 218 kg (481 lb) (ABS version 222 kg/489 lb)
Top speed
225 km/h (140 mph)

SUZUKI GSF 1250N BANDIT/GSF 1250SA BANDIT

Engine
1255 cc, liquid-cooled, fuel-injected, double-overhead-camshaft, four-cylinder, four-stroke
Power
72 kW (96 bhp) @ 7500 rpm
Torque
109 Nm (80 ft lb) @ 3700 rpm
Gearbox
Six-speed
Final drive
Chain
Weight
1250N, 225 kg (496 lb); 1250SA, 229 kg (505 lb)
Top speed
225 km/h (140 mph) (est.)

Suzuki's old Bandit 1200 has consistently been one of the most popular muscle machines on the market since it was launched in 1996, owing to a mix of classic, big-bike looks, bags of power and bullet-proof reliability. But ever-stricter emissions regulations have brought about the demise of the simple, air-and-oil-cooled Bandit, which has now been replaced by this larger-engined, liquid-cooled version.

Fortunately for the many Bandit lovers, the new bike retains all the character and some of the aesthetics of the old one, while also accomplishing the difficult task of providing even better low-down power, quieter running and generally enhanced performance.

But, despite its size, the Bandit isn't, and never has been, about huge power: even the new 1250 produces only 72 kW (96 bhp). But it is the way this is delivered that counts – in a strong, smooth curve of linear power that begins way down the rev range to provide relaxed cruising, tractor-like pulling ability and excellent fuel efficiency for its capacity.

Handling is surprisingly lithe, too, courtesy of an upgrade of the front forks and, in half-faired S guise, the bike makes an excellent touring machine in the old-fashioned style. Most buyers will probably go for the naked N version, however, because this follows more closely the muscle-bike tradition of mean looks and easy wheelies. The unfaired model also lends itself more readily to customization, a popular pastime among Bandit owners and one catered for by a vast after-market accessory industry.

SUZUKI

Bandit S

WAKAN

WAKAN
1
WAKAN

WAKAN
1

WAKAN

Wakan founder Joel Domergue built his first motorcycle at the age of fifteen and has spent the rest of his life as a serial modifier, designer and creator of peak-performance machines. After thirteen years of working in the French nuclear industry he established his first motorcycle company in 1993 to build trials bikes, an enterprise that was very successful and produced several championship-winning machines.

Domergue's lifelong aim, however, was to create a street motorcycle from scratch, so he sold the trials-bike firm and set up Wakan in the south of France. The result is what is seen here: a radical, minimal machine that is a symphony of swooping curves and sculptural, v-twin engine.

The strict design criteria were to produce a compact motorcycle with a fully exposed engine, a low centre of gravity, sharp handling, a forward riding position and an absolute maximum weight of 180 kg (397 lb). If all this sounds a little familiar, you are probably thinking that the Wakan is little more than a duplicate Buell, but you would be wrong.

For a start, the S & S performance engine displaces an impressively large 1640 cc and dominates the bike's extraordinarily short 137-cm (54-in.) wheelbase. The fuel cell is positioned beneath the seat, and the top of the convex dummy fuel tank houses the adjustable air intake that feeds a single, giant carburettor. The Ceriani front forks are angled at a steep 22 degrees, and carry a single front disc, which is perhaps not really adequate for a machine of the Wakan's performance potential.

'Road' and 'Racing' models are available, the second having a few track tweaks, such as a different exhaust system. The motorcycles from the first production run of a little more than one hundred machines are expected to be priced at around 28,000 euros each.

Engine
1640 cc, air-cooled, v-twin, four-stroke
Power
86 kW (115 bhp) @ 5000 rpm (est.)
Torque
156 Nm (115 ft lb) @ 4000 rpm
Gearbox
Five-speed
Final drive
Chain
Weight
177 kg (390 lb)
Top speed
225 km/h (140 mph) (est.)

YAMAHA FZ6 S2/ FZ6 S2 FAZER

Engine
598 cc, liquid-cooled, fuel-injected, double-overhead-camshaft, four-cylinder, four-stroke
Power
72 kW (98 bhp) @ 12,000 rpm
Torque
63 Nm (46 ft lb) @ 10,000 rpm
Gearbox
Six-speed
Final drive
Chain
Weight
FZ6 S2, 186 kg (410 lb) (ABS version 191 kg/ 421 lb); FZ6 S2 Fazer, 180 kg (397 lb) (ABS version 185 kg/408 lb)
Top speed
233 km/h (145 mph)

Yamaha's FZ 600-cc all-rounders have been Europe's best-selling middleweight machines for several years as a result of their sound build quality, reliability, ease of use and excellent performance. These latest S2 versions are powered by a second-generation engine from the R6 pure sports bike that has been retuned and fitted with a re-mapped fuel-injection system to make it more tractable and flexible for everyday use, while still giving an excellent turn of speed.

Handling is almost on a par with the sports bike, too, thanks to a lightweight, high-rigidity alloy frame that is now paired with an alloy swing arm incorporating an unusual hexagonal cross-section for extra rigidity. The S2-series machines additionally benefit from Yamaha's 'monobloc' brakes, which consist of a trio of compact and ultra-light brake calipers that are said to provide enhanced feel and sharper stopping power, with an anti-lock system being available as an optional extra.

The distinctive look of the FZ6 has also been altered, with the faired Fazer version getting a more 'attacking' front cowl inspired by the R-series supersports bikes, in order to accentuate its upgraded performance. A new screen cuts wind swirl and buffeting at high speed, while aerodynamics are further improved by a newly designed front mudguard that curves around the fork legs.

High-specification instruments have also been added, with the digital speedometer and analogue rev counter getting a back-lighting function to allow a choice of brilliance to suit conditions. But the way these lights 'fade in' when the ignition is switched on is pure gimmickry.

31
NEW BLUE
TITANIUM

RETRO

CCM

CCM CR-40

The British invented the idea of the café racer, in which a standard street bike is stripped of superfluous additions and fitted with lightweight mudguards, rear-set footrests, a single seat, and race-style handlebars. So it seems entirely appropriate that the true-Brit marque CCM should have produced the authentically retro CR-40.

Had this motorcycle pitched up at London's Ace Cafe fifty years ago, it would not, at first glance, have looked out of place: the polished-alloy fuel tank, the big, single-cylinder engine, the megaphone exhaust and the humped seat were all prerequisites of a decent home-built race replica back then, and they're all on the CR-40 now. But once the crowds began to take a closer look, they would see that CCM has cleverly combined old and new by fitting the bike with a liquid-cooled Suzuki engine to make it go and a powerful Grimeca braking system at the front to make it stop.

While the CR-40 produces just 31 kW (42 bhp) and struggles to exceed 137 km/h (85 mph), its lightness makes for impeccable handling, and the sound of the 'thumper' engine is just as evocative no matter how fast you're going. This is a bike to ride along country lanes on warm summer evenings, on which to potter about town and, above all, one with which to travel back in time.

Sales should be steady on CCM's home ground, but it is likely that the CR-40 will attract just as much, if not more, attention from the country that almost destroyed Britain's motorcycle industry back in the 1970s. For the Japanese, more than any other nation, have embraced café-racer culture, and for them the more retro the better.

Engine
398 cc, liquid-cooled, double-overhead-camshaft, single-cylinder, four-valve, four-stroke
Power
31 kW (42 bhp) @ 7000 rpm
Torque
39 Nm (29 ft lb) @ 5000 rpm
Gearbox
Five-speed
Final drive
Chain
Weight
122 kg (269 lb)
Top speed
137 km/h (85 mph)

CROCKER

Engine
1000 cc, hemispherical-head v-twin, four-stroke
Power
41 kW (55 bhp) @ 6500 rpm (est.)
Torque
N/A
Gearbox
Three-speed
Final drive
Chain
Weight
215 kg (475 lb)
Top speed
169 km/h (105 mph)

You will have noticed that this book concentrates largely on new production motorcycles, most from well-known manufacturers, but occasionally a very special creation built in tiny numbers also deserves a place within these pages. One such bike is the Crocker, although in order to own one you'll need to be prepared to do a little work.

The Crocker Motorcycle Company of Toronto, Canada, is an extraordinary operation that is dedicated to the memory of an extraordinary man, the late Al Crocker, a brilliant engineer who founded his eponymous motorcycle marque back in the early 1930s. Only about a hundred examples of his 1000-cc, v-twin touring machine were built before production ceased in 1941, but every one was meticulously assembled and virtually tailor-made for its owner. Each could top 161 km/h (100 mph) and, at $600, cost $100 more than a comparable motorcycle from the rival Harley-Davidson marque.

In recent years the value of these bikes has soared – a good example is now worth around $300,000 – and, as more 'lost' Crockers began to emerge, the Crocker Motorcycle Company was formed in 1997 to provide history, technical information and, most importantly, new components that would enable the owners of run-down Crockers to restore them to perfection.

The beauty of these parts is that, while they are interchangeable with their relevant originals, they are made with modern materials and tooling and to the far closer tolerances now possible thanks to CAM (Computer-Aided Machining). In other words, they are better than even the great Al Crocker could have made them.

And, since the Crocker Motorcycle Company is capable of producing or supplying every component required to create a new machine, you can build your own, zero-mileage Crocker from a $50,000 kit if you're prepared to piece all the bits together from scratch. If you do, and you love retro bikes, you won't be disappointed. For the Crocker was a legendary bike, and the fact that, after more than sixty years, the name has been revived from the ashes to ride again is fitting tribute to its status.

CROCKER

HARLEY-DAVIDSON
1200
5

HARLEY-DAVIDSON NIGHTSTER

In the late 1970s, Harley-Davidson launched an achingly cool motorcycle called the XLX61. It had a single saddle, pull-back handlebars and large, protruding air filters. I desperately wanted one, but for an impecunious teenager there was no chance whatsoever of that.

Now, thirty years on, H-D has produced a remarkably similar-looking machine (albeit without the protruding air filters) that is based on a stripped-down Sportster 1200 with some nice detail touches to give it a mean, retro-street look.

With a short rear mudguard, such 'machined' components as the drive-belt guard and the front mudguard brackets, and a lustrous black finish to such parts as the wheel rims, fork legs and handlebars, it looks very much like a factory-built version of the home-made 'bobbers' that backyard customizers created from former War Department Harleys during the 1950s. In fact, the marque's designers admit that they went out of their way to make this bike look illegal!

Rubber fork gaiters, a side-mounted number-plate bracket and stubby, slash-cut exhausts all add to the old-fashioned personality, although the engine has all the benefits of modern engineering, such as the latest electronic fuel injection and Harley's new, slicker-shifting gearbox.

All in all, it's my dream v-twin street bike all over again – and, three decades later, I still can't afford it.

Engine
1202 cc, v-twin, four-stroke
Power
63 kW (85 bhp) @ 5000 rpm (est.)
Torque
107 Nm (79 ft lb) @ 4000 rpm
Gearbox
Five-speed
Final drive
Belt
Weight
247 kg (545 lb)
Top speed
193 km/h (120 mph) (est.)

MECATWIN TRIUMPH BONNEVILLE SPRINGFIELD

Engine
865 cc, air-cooled, parallel-twin, double-overhead-camshaft, eight-valve, four-stroke
Power
59 kW (79 bhp) @ 8000 rpm (est.)
Torque
75 Nm (55 ft lb) @ 6200 rpm (est.)
Gearbox
Five-speed
Final drive
Chain
Weight
193 kg (425 lb)
Top speed
193 km/h (120 mph)

The modern version of Triumph's legendary parallel twin readily lends itself to customization, and nowadays many European and American companies specialize in building 'Bonnies' with an even more classic look than the one with which they leave the factory. Some, such as Germany's LSL, even carry out extensive modifications to chassis and engine to make the bike go better than any 1950s café racer ever did.

But it seems to be the French who have mastered the art of Bonneville customization better than anyone. For proof, look at the Mecatwin Springfield flat tracker shown here. The bike has a performance upgrade kit that boosts power by an impressive 20 per cent over standard, and by replacing several standard Triumph components with lightweight items, or leaving them off altogether, Mecatwin has cut the Springfield's dry weight from around 205 kg (452 lb) to 193 kg (425 lb).

Other significant changes include exchanging the original two-sided exhaust system for a stacked version that exits on the right of the bike; the replacement of standard Triumph handlebars with a wider, flat-track-style pattern; and the fitting of semi-knobbly tyres similar to those used on Triumph's Bonneville Scrambler. The rear of the bike has also been tidied up: it now has a small tail light and a truncated mudguard beneath the seat cowl.

The overall effect is to make the Springfield look as though it has just been prepared for a 1960s-style desert race – one can easily imagine Steve McQueen leaping aboard and powering it through the sand dunes.

CATWIN
Springfield

31
NEW BLUE
DUCATI NCR
NCR

31
NEW BLUE
NCR

NCR NEW BLUE

You can learn about the history of the Italian race-bike builder NCR in the Sports section of this book (pp. 38–39), while here you can see how the company that is best known for its high-tech upgrades of Ducati competition bikes has created a stunning retro machine based on the new SportClassic Sport1000.

New Blue is a tuned version of the stock bike that produces an extra 22 kW (30 bhp) of power and weighs around 36 kg (80 lb) less. It was built in homage to the celebrated 1970s racers Cook Neilson and Phil Schilling, who campaigned a blue-and-silver Ducati 750SS named Old Blue around US circuits, competing at a disadvantage against contemporary Japanese four-cylinder superbikes that had lesser handling but far greater power.

Neilson and Schilling kept Old Blue in the running by tuning the engine with after-market parts originally designed for hot-rodding cars, as there were few purpose-built, high-performance components available for the Ducati unit. The team's David-and-Goliath efforts finally paid off with their most celebrated victory, which came in an AMA Superbike race at Daytona Speedway – the first time a Ducati had won at the famous circuit.

New Blue was the brainchild of Ducati North America's boss, Michael Lock, who commissioned NCR to upgrade a 2007 Sport1000 by tuning the engine and fitting a Zard exhaust system, better suspension and radial brakes. The finishing touch, of course, was to apply a blue-and-silver paint job, just like that of the original. A limited number of New Blues will be built for the American market.

Engine
992 cc, air-cooled, l-twin, eight-valve, four-stroke
Power
91 kW (122 bhp) @ 8500 rpm (est.)
Torque
95 Nm (70 ft lb) @ 6200 rpm
Gearbox
Six-speed
Final drive
Chain
Weight
159 kg (350 lb) (est.)
Top speed
225 km/h (140 mph)

ROYAL ENFIELD BULLET ELECTRA XS/BULLET ELECTRA CLUBMAN

Engine
499 cc, overhead valve, single-cylinder, four-stroke
Power
21 kW (28 bhp) @ 5500 rpm
Torque
47 Nm (35 ft lb) @ 3500 rpm
Gearbox
Five-speed
Final drive
Chain
Weight
187 kg (412 lb)
Top speed
137 km/h (85 mph)

As the world's oldest surviving motorcycle maker, Royal Enfield doesn't need to invent its retro credentials. The Bullet, its core model, has been in continuous production since Enfield Motors India began making it under licence for that country's army. The Indian plant continued to thrive after the UK factory closed in 1970, and in 1994 Enfield India was bought by the giant engineering group Eicher, which has since invested in it heavily.

Without Eicher the brand might have disappeared, because, although there has always been a steady demand for the Bullet, modern emissions regulations made the original engine design unviable. As a result, a new lean-burn unit was recently introduced and, while the 'Classic' models with cast-iron engines, four-speed gearboxes and right-foot gear change will remain available for a few more months, the latest bikes have five-speed gearboxes, disc brakes and electric starters.

The Electra XS is the latest take on the Bullet theme. It has the modern, all-alloy engine and is equipped with flat handlebars, sporty chrome mudguards and an upswept exhaust system. A significant change, however, is that the instruments that were traditionally housed in the headlamp nacelle have now been replaced by twin, chromed units for recording speed and engine revs.

Handling has been improved, too, with gas-filled shock absorbers and high-quality Avon tyres. But the look remains as genuinely retro as it always has done, and the versatility of the Bullet is demonstrated by the fact that it is also available in 'Clubman' and 'Sportsman' café-racer guise, trials trim and as a tourer in the form of the 500 GT.

ROYAL
ENFIELD

SCOOTER AND MAXI SCOOTER

agv
SPEEDY

BAOTIAN QT50

Looking for an excuse to take to two wheels? This could be it, if only for its absurdly small price tag: the Baotian QT50 costs just £695 in the United Kingdom (even less in some other countries). That's a mere third of the price of an entry-level Yamaha Neos 50, yet it starts, goes and stops just as well. The only question marks relate to the Chinese-built Baotian's long-term reliability and longevity. A bike as cheap to buy as this is inevitably built down to its price, and that means that you get no fancy components, just the basics sourced from the least expensive manufacturers.

The Baotian is not, however, the clanging, smoking two-stroke you would expect at such a price; instead it is powered by a surprisingly sprightly four-stroke engine that, in unrestricted form, is good enough to give a top speed of 72 km/h (45 mph). This little machine is also extraordinarily well equipped, being fitted with a top box, electronic immobilizer and even a crude anti-lock braking system as standard.

Another reason why all this can be offered so cheaply is that at present there is no chance of finding a Baotian dealer on your local high street, although a network is in the making. This scooter can be bought only via the Internet, being delivered direct from the importer ready to roll, with everything fitted and all fluids, apart from fuel, already added. There is, however, a comprehensive back-up system for spares.

So what's stopping you?

Engine
49 cc, air-cooled, single-cylinder, four-stroke
Power
2 kW (3 bhp) @ 600 rpm
Torque
4 Nm (3 ft lb) @ 5000 rpm
Gearbox
Automatic
Final drive
Direct
Weight
85 kg (187 lb)
Top speed
48 km/h (30 mph); 72 km/h (45 mph) unrestricted

CF MOTO V3

Gilera's hot new GP800 super scooter (pp. 196–97) hints that automatic motorcycles, as opposed to scooters, may be the next two-wheeled trend to hit the streets, but has CF Moto got there already with its V3? Well, it has all the look of a scooter/motorcycle hybrid, but to my eye it's more like the second, and the engine is mounted under the seat (almost like a motorcycle) rather than towards the back (like a scooter), so perhaps the answer is yes.

It will come as no surprise that the innovative Chinese build this bike, but, while imaginative and well equipped, it will be no match for the competition from Japanese and European manufacturers should they catch on to auto motorcycles. Despite the 'V3' tag, there is nothing more exciting than a cooking, 250-cc, four-stroke single under the semi-cruiser-style plastic bodywork, but the machine does make up for its old-fashioned mechanicals with the addition of a combined radio, cassette and MP3 player to help ease the monotony of the daily commute.

Performance-wise, this is a low-powered scooter that weighs as much as a middleweight Japanese sports bike, so prepare not to be startled. Top speed is around 121 km/h (75 mph), and braking is handled by the most basic set-up of a single disc front and rear. A low centre of gravity and full-sized motorbike wheels make it nicely manoeuvrable, but non-adjustable front forks and shock absorbers mean that the handling characteristics are determined more by the rider's weight than by the suspension set-up.

For those torn between buying a motorcycle or a scooter, the CF Moto is currently the only way to enjoy the best of both worlds; but probably not for long.

Engine
244 cc, liquid-cooled, single-cylinder, four-stroke
Power
11 kW (15 bhp) @ 7000 rpm (est.)
Torque
18 Nm (13 ft lb) @ 6000 rpm (est.)
Gearbox
Automatic
Final drive
Belt
Weight
177 kg (390 lb)
Top speed
121 km/h (75 mph)

CF250T-3

GILERA GP800

Look at Gilera's maxi scooter at a certain angle from the front and it could almost be a 322-km/h (200-mph) Suzuki Hayabusa. In fact, this supersports machine can lay claim to being the fastest, most powerful scooter yet offered for sale, thanks to a v-twin, 56-kW (75-bhp) engine of almost 850 cc that propels it to a top speed of 187 km/h (116 mph).

The very existence of the GP800 seems to point the way towards the inevitable arrival of a large-capacity twist-and-go motorcycle, but until that appears (and I suspect we'll be writing about one next year) this is essentially a scooter with performance approaching that of a conventional motorcycle such as the Ducati Monster 600 or the Suzuki SV650.

The 90-degree v-twin engine is, of course, liquid-cooled and fuel-injected and produces the type of torque that will enable the GP800 to beat many a superbike or supercar away from the lights and to hold its own in the motorway fast lane. The bodywork has been designed to combine practicality with aggressive, sporting looks, an image enhanced by the scooter's fat, 41-cm (16-in.) rear tyre, slim back end, twin-silencer exhaust system and wrap-around frame – just like that of a contemporary sports bike.

With two 300-mm (11.8-in.) front discs and a pair of race-style Brembo brake calipers, the GP800 has eye-popping stopping power and, thanks to its lightweight aluminium wheels and alloy front forks, sharp handling. Its sporting credentials are further emphasized by an innovative transmission that offers a choice of modes, including a seven-speed, semi-automatic setting for maximum performance. An enhanced engine-braking effect, usually absent from twist-and-go machines, has also been engineered into the transmission.

Any chance of a race series, Gilera?

Engine
839 cc, liquid-cooled, overhead-camshaft, 90-degree v-twin, four-stroke
Power
56 kW (75 bhp) @ 7250 rpm
Torque
76 Nm (56 ft lb) @ 5750 rpm
Gearbox
Automatic with mode selection
Final drive
Belt
Weight
235 kg (518 lb)
Top speed
187 km/h (116 mph)

HONDA FORZA SMART 2-SEATER

Specifications not available

This vehicle was one of four concepts unveiled by Honda at the 2007 Tokyo Motor Show, and it seems highly likely that by the time you read this it (or something similar) will be part of Honda's line-up. The USPs of this eye-catching machine are its exceptional level of comfort and its portable AVN system.

'AVN' stands for 'audiovisual navigation', a high-quality entertainment system and rider-to-passenger intercom that is linked with a state-of-the-art satellite-navigation unit. The theory behind the Forza Smart 2-Seater is that it should be owned as an urban convenience vehicle in conjunction with another of Honda's prototype machines, the equally strangely named Fit Daily Active. As a result, body and seating colour schemes are co-ordinated and the AVN system can be moved from one to the other without the need for any reprogramming. Like its four-wheeled stablemate, the Forza boasts LED headlights and front fog lights, automatic 'welcome' lighting and a passenger backrest that incorporates a high-visibility stop lamp.

The Forza Smart underlines the fact that scooters are increasingly being seen as an essential accessory; something that every household will eventually need to own in order to have motorized transport that is relatively immune to the growing congestion of our cities. Honda clearly believes that it will be able to seize a major part of this prospective market by making powered two-wheelers that will prove acceptable to a generation that has grown up with the cocooned environment of the car.

HONDA

HONDA SH300i

Elsewhere in this book we trace the rise of Honda's motorcycle operation from its small beginnings to the giant it is today (see pp.14–17). An important step on that journey was the introduction in the 1950s of the now ubiquitous Super Cub, a simple, no-frills, large-wheeled scooter with leg shields and three-speed, clutchless transmission. So far, fifty million have been sold.

Looking at Honda's latest large-engined scooter, the luxurious SH300i, it is easy to see the Super Cub lineage in the design silhouette, but this fast, ultra-refined machine is in a different league altogether. Boasting the best acceleration in its class, the SH300i can hit 113 km/h (70 mph) with ease and, more importantly, remain smooth and rock-steady all the way. This is all down to its neutral handling and a beautifully balanced, fuel-injected and liquid-cooled engine that is quiet, virtually vibration-free and remarkably compact, thanks to a sealed crankcase construction that eliminates the need for an oil sump.

Anti-lock braking, large-diameter wheels, a linked braking system and good looks also help make this a scooter that even dyed-in-the-wool motorcyclists would be happy to own as a second, practical two-wheeler.

And practicality was clearly high on the agenda when Honda's engineers designed this capable little machine. The flat footboard area takes shopping bags and makes it easy to get on and off the seat (especially for women in skirts); additional space for luggage is provided in the traditional underseat storage area; and the waterproof glove-box contains a DC socket so that mobile phones and hand-held computers can be charged on the move.

Engine
279 cc, liquid-cooled, overhead-camshaft, single-cylinder, four-valve, four-stroke
Power
20 kW (27 bhp) @ 8250 rpm
Torque
26 Nm (19 ft lb) @ 6000 rpm
Gearbox
Automatic
Final drive
Belt
Weight
162 kg (357 lb)
Top speed
121 km/h (75 mph)

PEUGEOT SATELIS 250

Engine
249 cc, liquid-cooled, fuel-injected, overhead-camshaft, single-cylinder, four-stroke
Power
16 kW (22 bhp) @ 7500 rpm
Torque
18 Nm (13 ft lb) @ 6500 rpm
Gearbox
Automatic
Final drive
Direct
Weight
160 kg (353 lb)
Top speed
137 km/h (85 mph)

Peugeot's powered two-wheeler division made its name with the trendy Speedfight two-stroke machines, which topped the scooter bestseller list for years. Gradually, however, Peugeot 'Motocycles' (as the firm calls them) have well and truly come of age and now cater as much for pinstriped commuters as for teenagers who want the coolest wheels in town.

The first serious attempts at luxury, fully faired scooters were the Elystar and Elyseo models of the late 1990s, but these seem positively agricultural in comparison with the new Satelis, which is equipped with a range of features and a level of performance that, a decade ago, would have seemed unimaginable on a machine of this size.

Peugeot's first 250-cc offering, the Satelis, produces a useful 16 kW (22 bhp), which gives it sharp acceleration in town and sufficient urge to reach maximum speed on the open road. It's a perfect scooter for a daily ride to work of 30–50 km (20–30 miles). The large fairing with integrated leg shields keeps the worst of the elements at bay when travelling at motorway speeds, but it isn't just beneficial for weather protection, as its carefully engineered wind-tunnel design has given the machine an exceptionally low drag coefficient that helps it return a combined fuel consumption of over 23 kmpl (65 mpg).

Less-experienced riders will be drawn to the safety provided by the excellent anti-lock braking system, which was first offered on the old Elyseo. The Satelis version has been refined and is virtually unnoticeable in operation, even when the system is having to work hard on loose or slippery surfaces.

Owners used to the comfort and convenience of a car will also appreciate the capacious 'boot' (easily capable of swallowing a full-face crash helmet), which is accessed by raising the pillion seat. This is sensibly equipped with oil-damped struts, which remove the need to hold up the lid when loading. Further underlining the practical nature of the Satelis, each machine is supplied with a sturdy security chain to keep it in the hands of its rightful owner.

SATELIS

Carnaby
PIAGGIO

Piaggio's new Carnaby is the latest in a line of so-called 'high-wheel' scooters that have found popularity with novice riders thanks to their greater stability compared with smaller-wheeled machines. Intended to be midway between the firm's compact Liberty and the semi-touring Beverly, the Carnaby is a simple, no-nonsense machine that is aimed at people who are not necessarily fans of powered two-wheelers but simply want to get from A to B as conveniently as possible.

The flat footboard is typical of the latest machines in this class. Uninterrupted by the bulge of an underslung frame tube, it makes it easier both to carry bags and to mount and dismount. Piaggio's modellers have also tried hard to give the Carnaby 'personality', much in the way that the designers of the Mini and VW Beetle did, by providing it with a friendly-looking frontal appearance and an attractive, two-tone seat unit that is covered in heat-reflective upholstery.

The machine is low to the ground and its handlebars are wide – both features that enhance its gridlock-busting capabilities and make it easier for beginners to handle. Other practical touches include underseat helmet storage, side panels that double as compartments for gloves, telephones and the like, a removable carry bag tailored to the front shield compartment and an 'anti-skid', easy-lift stand.

To reduce the misery of commuting in winter, the Carnaby is even supplied with a heated, fold-away cover that channels warm air from the radiator to the rider's legs.

PIAGGIO CARNABY 125/CARNABY 200

Engine
198 cc or 124 cc, liquid-cooled, single-cylinder, four-valve, four-stroke
Power
15 kW (20 bhp) @ 9000 rpm (198); 11 kW (15 bhp) @ 9750 rpm (124)
Torque
21 Nm (15 ft lb) @ 6250 rpm (198); 12 Nm (9 ft lb) @ 8000 rpm (124)
Gearbox
Automatic
Final drive
Direct
Weight
146 kg (322 lb)
Top speed
121 km/h (75 mph) (198); 100 km/h (62 mph) (124)

SUZUKI BURGMAN 125

Engine
125 cc, liquid-cooled, overhead-camshaft, single-cylinder, four-stroke
Power
9 kW (12 bhp) (est.)
Torque
N/A
Gearbox
Automatic
Final drive
Direct
Weight
148 kg (326 lb)
Top speed
105 km/h (65 mph)

Suzuki claims that 'total urban coolness' defines the design of the Burgman 125. And with competition hotting up in the small-to-mid-sized scooter market, image is undoubtedly all-important, for there is very little to choose from between one offering from Japan or Italy and another, other than that Japanese scooters tend to have the edge in terms of reliability and longevity.

This 125-cc machine is the entry-level scooter in the Burgman range, which also includes 400- and 650-cc models. Like the Yamaha X-Max, it is scaled down in all departments but still offers excellent comfort, weather protection and storage facilities. The size of its engine, however, makes it only really suitable for the urban environment for which it was designed. Long-distance commuters are advised to opt for a larger, more powerful alternative.

The liquid-cooled, four-stroke engine is tuned to provide maximum low-down torque, which is exactly what is required for the 'traffic-light grand prix' in which machines such as this compete each working day. The seat is nice and low, making the Burgman an ideal choice for shorter riders, and comes with an integrated pillion backrest as standard.

Other practical features include the illuminated underseat storage space, which will take two full-face helmets. The Burgman is also equipped with what has, unfortunately, become almost essential: a lockable ignition compartment with a magnetic security cover, which will at least reduce the chances of the machine ending up a burned-out wreck.

BURGMAN 125

VESPA S

The youth of today may not care much about *La Dolce Vita* or Gregory Peck squiring Audrey Hepburn in *Roman Holiday*. Even so, Piaggio believes they would still like a taste of the Italy of the 1950s, and that is why it has produced the Vespa S: a twenty-first-century take on the sporty, minimalist machines that were part of the line-up before scooters fell from favour in the late 1970s.

The reduced handlebars on the Vespa S complement a retro rectangular headlamp, and the scooter has been given a more aggressive look, with a larger leg shield fitted with an air scoop. In addition, the front mudguard now has a dash of chrome and has been minimized to give a better view of the suspension and light alloy wheel. The 'less is more' theme is continued at the back, with sleek engine covers and a neat new tail light. There are two seat options: single and racy or twin and practical. Both are finished in a new upholstery design.

Modern emissions regulations demanded that the crackling, smoking two-stroke engines that contributed to the character of the original Vespa models be replaced with environmentally friendly powerplants. The 49-cc S has a hairdryer-like two-stroke engine and the 125 a purring four-stroke.

Engine
49 cc, single-cylinder, two-stroke; or 125 cc, single-cylinder, four-stroke
Power
49 cc, not available; 125 cc, 7 kW (10 bhp) @ 8000 rpm
Torque
49 cc, not available; 125 cc, 10 Nm (7 ft lb) @ 6000 rpm
Gearbox
Automatic
Final drive
Direct
Weight
49 cc, 96 kg (212 lb); 125 cc, 110 kg (243 lb)
Top speed
49 cc, 48 km/h (30 mph); 125 cc, 105 km/h (65 mph)

YAMAHA GIGGLE

The first edition of *The New Motorcycle Yearbook* featured Honda's then new – and revolutionary – Zoomer 'street culture' scooter, which was designed to take the knocks and scrapes of urban life and even carry your skateboard. Yamaha's even cooler take on the theme is the Giggle: a scooter that, with its chunky tyres, boxy bodywork and almost industrial appearance, is reminiscent of the Bauhaus 'form follows function' approach to design.

Back in the mid-1990s Yamaha produced a similarly trend-setting machine called the BW that became a favourite among teenagers, and the Giggle seems set to take its place. Fat, multi-purpose tyres offer grip in on- and off-road conditions, there is an impressive 33 litres (1.2 cu. ft) of storage space beneath the seat, and the slabby, angular lines of the bodywork should stand up well to the abuse this little machine is likely to receive at the hands of its young owners.

The Giggle is mechanically interesting, too, as it is fitted with Yamaha's first attempt at a 50-cc, four-stroke engine. This state-of-the-art liquid-cooled, overhead-camshaft unit is tilted forward in the frame to keep the centre of gravity as low as possible. Electronic fuel injection ensures reliable starting and astounding fuel economy of up to 72 kmpl (200 mpg) and, with a mere 87 kg (192 lb) to pull, the Giggle feels as brisk as any other '50' on the market.

Engine
49 cc, liquid-cooled, fuel-injected, overhead-camshaft, single-cylinder, three-valve, four-stroke
Power
2 kW (3 bhp) @ 6000 rpm
Torque
3 Nm (2 ft lb) @ 5500 rpm
Gearbox
Automatic
Final drive
Direct
Weight
87 kg (192 lb)
Top speed
56 km/h (35 mph)

YAMAHA

YAMAHA X-MAX 250

With the exception of the iconic Vespa, scooters were at one time something to feel slightly ashamed of. Back when traffic conditions were not as hellish as they are in most cities today, riding a scooter normally indicated a lack of funds to buy a decent motorbike or a small car. But now that a scooter has become the logical tool for getting around for any self-respecting man or woman about town, it has become as much an essential accessory as the latest pair of designer sunglasses, hand-made shoes or must-have handbag.

Yamaha has capitalized on this cultural change by making the X-Max one of the best-looking mid-sized scooters on the market. Based on its bigger brother, the T-Max 500, it adopts the half-litre machine's large-diameter wheels in a lighter, shorter package that is ideally suited to town work. At the same time, the 250-cc engine packs sufficient punch to make the X-Max a practical proposition for moderate out-of-town and motorway use. Excellent underseat storage space provides plenty of room for shopping or, for the pillion-passenger carrier, two full-face helmets.

Engine
249 cc, liquid-cooled, fuel-injected, single-cylinder, four-stroke
Power
24 kW (32 bhp) @ 7500 rpm
Torque
21 Nm (15 ft lb) @ 6250 rpm
Gearbox
Automatic
Final drive
Direct
Weight
164 kg (362 lb)
Top speed
121 km/h (75 mph)

ODDBALL

can-am
990

can-am

CAN-AM SPYDER

A glance through this section will reveal that several designers are turning their attention to the development of three-wheeled motorcycles. The Can-Am Spyder is probably the most radical of the lot, being powered by a 990-cc engine similar to that of Aprilia's Mille R superbike.

The thinking behind the Spyder is that it provides all the thrills of a first-rate sports bike with some of the safety of a sports car, and just as much care has been taken to make it idiot-proof as to make it look radically attractive. In addition to now commonplace safety aids such as anti-lock braking and traction control, it boasts EBD (electronic brake distribution), VSS (vehicle stability system), SCS (an anti-roll function), and DPS (dynamic power steering).

Other silicon-chip trickery will include an optional, electronically controlled gearbox similar to that found on factory racing cars and motorcycles.

Surprisingly, the Spyder is not expected to cost much more than a medium-range superbike, such as a Honda Fireblade or Suzuki GSX-R1000, despite its plethora of high-tech wizardry and, of course, the fact that it has a third wheel. It strikes me as a machine that I would love to borrow for a long weekend in order to put it through its paces on a pristine mountain road, but when it comes to the Monday-morning commute, that car-wide front end might prove awfully frustrating.

Engine
990 cc, liquid-cooled, double-overhead-camshaft, v-twin, eight-valve, four-stroke
Power
79 kW (106 bhp) @ 8500 rpm
Torque
104 Nm (77 ft lb) @ 6250 rpm
Gearbox
Six-speed
Final drive
Belt
Weight
316 kg (697 lb)
Top speed
209 km/h (130 mph) (est.)

eCYCLE eC1/2/3

Machineart is an industrial-design company based in New Jersey, United States, that carries out projects ranging from creating radical new bodywork for production motorcycles to providing one-off, modified and customized machines for film and promotional use.

A series of three machines for the American client eCycle is Machineart's look into the future of powered two-wheelers. It started with the eC1, an urban-orientated machine that, in terms of looks, was inspired by Honda's Super Cub of the 1960s. In engineering terms, however, the eC1 and its brethren the eC2 (sports) and eC3 (commuter) could scarcely be more different from the conventional Cub. All three are designed with an interesting modular, asymmetrical chassis layout that is supported at the front by a swing-arm suspension system and at the rear by a conventional monoshock.

The seat and the fuel tank flow together, and the handlebar area and instrumentation are extremely minimal, but what would make the eCycle machines really different if they ever went into production is the fact that they are intended to combine electricity with petrol power by having a brushless motor that is run from an on-board generator.

Machineart believes that the combination would give 129-km/h (80-mph) performance combined with fuel consumption better than 54 kmpl (150 mpg). It sounds great, so let's hope it gets off the drawing board.

Specifications not available

ec1
eCycle
machineart

eCycle
ec3
machineart

ec2
eCycle
machineart

GILERA FUOCO

Elsewhere in this section you can discover the Piaggio MP3 (see pp. 230–31), and this machine from Gilera (another part of the Piaggio group) is the high-performance take on the same three-wheeled theme. Aggressive and sporty-looking, the Fuoco, meaning 'fire', is marketed as a way of having 'safe fun' because, like the Piaggio MP3, it is theoretically harder to crash than a normal two-wheeled scooter.

The rugged appearance is enhanced by the steel-tube front 'bumper' and mesh inserts, together with off-road tyres and ten-spoke wheels finished in a moody black. The headlamp unit contains no fewer than five lenses, two of them protected by stone guards.

But does Gilera really expect anyone to ride this machine on the dirt? The answer is probably no, although ironically the twin front wheels do provide excellent grip on loose and slippery surfaces. So the Fuoco would most likely be a joy to throw around a gentle off-road track, particularly since it can reach 150 km/h (93 mph), thanks to its 500-cc, fuel-injected engine.

Engine
492 cc, liquid-cooled, fuel-injected, single-cylinder, four-stroke
Power
30 kW (40 bhp) @ 7000 rpm
Torque
42 Nm (31 ft lb) @ 5500 rpm
Gearbox
Automatic
Final drive
Direct
Weight
238 kg (525 lb)
Top speed
150 km/h (93 mph)

HONDA MONKEY 40TH ANNIVERSARY

Engine
49 cc, air-cooled, single-cylinder, four-stroke
Power
2 kW (3 bhp) @ 6000 rpm
Torque
N/A
Gearbox
Three-speed semi-automatic
Final drive
Chain
Weight
41 kg (90 lb) (est.)
Top speed
56 km/h (35 mph)

The true origins of Honda's legendary Monkey are not entirely certain, but it is believed that this cult machine was born after a group of student engineers at the Honda factory was tasked to produce a fun mini-motorcycle that could be fitted into the boot of a car and taken along on picnics, days at the beach and family outings. It would have to be small enough to be easily transportable, yet capable of carrying an adult.

The first production Monkey went on sale in 1963, but the quintessential version was the Z50M, launched four years later. It had fold-up handlebars, an adjustable seat, Honda's already ubiquitous 49-cc, four-stroke engine, chunky off-road tyres and a riding position that was more comfortable for Western-sized 'grown-ups'. The bike proved an instant hit, becoming the favoured means of transport in the pit lanes of the world's circuits and as an on-shore runabout for the yachting fraternity.

Interest in the Honda Monkey waned after the late 1970s, but enthusiasm suddenly began to grow again around fifteen years ago, and now it has an international following among both collectors of original models and riders of new ones. There are even tuning and customizing kits, and race and rally meetings are regularly staged throughout the world.

Honda has now produced this eye-catching 40th-Anniversary version to mark four decades since the arrival of the Z50M. It sports a 1960s-style tartan seat and a special black-and-red colour scheme, and comes with anniversary decals and a specially enamelled key. Ideal for a spot of monkey business.

HONDA

MONKEY
40

MANTISBIKES.C

MANTIS PRV

No edition of *The New Motorcycle Yearbook* would be complete without introducing a lightweight 'fun' bike designed for stunting and off-road antics. In the past we have given you the Sachs Madass, the Yamaha Tricker and the ElectricMoto Blade T6, and here we present the Canadian-built Mantis PRV, described by the company's founder and award-winning designer Stefan Marshall as a hybrid of bicycle and motocrosser.

Currently just a concept, the Mantis should be fairly straightforward to put into production, simply because it is very basic. With an aluminium box-section frame and single-sided fork and swing arm, the bike's structure is essentially based on just three parts. The prototype is powered by a 50-cc Honda generator engine that is required to propel an all-up weight of just 30 kg (66 lb). So one strong arm is all that is needed to lift the Mantis clean into the air, and, even set on terra firma, it offers an impressive 43.2 cm (17 in.) of ground clearance.

Another unconventional feature is the routing of the drive chain. Instead of being fitted on a horizontal plane, it is angled upwards at about 30 degrees to an engine drive sprocket mounted beneath the seat, which in turn is directly attached to a single, beefy shock absorber.

Lovers of fun bikes are already said to be praying that the Mantis reaches production.

Specifications not available

MARTIN CONQUEST

Engine
1130 cc, twin-cylinder, eight-valve, four-stroke
Power
62 kW (83 bhp) @ 6750 rpm
Torque
98 Nm (72 ft lb) @ 5250 rpm
Gearbox
Six-speed plus reverse
Final drive
Shaft
Weight
565 kg (1246 lb)
Top speed
161 km/h (100 mph)

Suffering from a serious disability does not have to mean being denied the thrill of motorcycling, and for decades ingenious enthusiasts have been devising adaptations to make riding possible even for those who are missing a limb. But British engineer Alan Martin's creation is the first high-performance trike designed specifically to be driven by wheelchair users.

This brilliantly made, cleverly conceived machine incorporates an electric ramp that allows the rider to drive up to the controls in his or her wheelchair, lock it into place, raise the ramp, and take to the road just as though they were riding a conventional motorcycle. The ramp is raised and lowered by an automatic control, and an interlock system prevents the Conquest from being driven off if the wheelchair is not properly secured.

Based on BMW mechanicals, the Conquest provides exhilarating performance and, despite the extra weight caused by the adaptations for wheelchair use, it can still accelerate from standstill to 97 km/h (60 mph) in 7.6 seconds. The gearbox is fitted with a reverse ratio, and up and down changes are carried out manually. There is a keyless entry system and an independent handbrake. A powerful CD player comes as standard, while the wide choice of extras embraces custom paintwork, twin luggage racks and a sports wheelchair.

In some countries the Martin Conquest is eligible for purchase under government-sponsored disability vehicle schemes. It's a wonderful creation that makes motorcycling possible for those who may never have expected to experience it.

PERAVES MONOTRACER

Is this the motorcycle of the future? Who knows, but it will certainly be of considerable appeal to anyone who does much winter riding, thanks to its fully enclosed design. You can read all about the prehistory, concept and creation of the Monotracer in a profile of its designer, Arnold Wagner (see pp. 248–251), but these photographs will tell you that it is unusual, to say the least.

Powered by BMW's 1200-cc, four-cylinder sports-bike engine, the Monotracer has dramatic acceleration and long-distance cruising capability as well as surprisingly agile handling. Those secondary wheels, incidentally, are to protect the bodywork at extreme lean angles, or on occasions when, as the rider/driver glides to a halt, he or she has forgotten to deploy the booms to which these wheels are attached.

The aerodynamic 'fuselage' gives the Monotracer a top speed of around 241 km/h (150 mph), but also enables it to be extremely frugal: ridden gently, it will easily deliver 21.6 kmpl (60 mpg). At 50,000 euros, however, it is a lot more expensive than the high-end sports-touring BMW on which it is based.

Engine
1157 cc, liquid-cooled, double-overhead-camshaft, four-cylinder, sixteen-valve, four-stroke
Power
113 kW (152 bhp) @ 9500 rpm
Torque
136 Nm (100 ft lb) @ 7750 rpm
Gearbox
Six-speed
Final drive
Shaft
Weight
460 kg (1014 lb)
Top Speed
241 km/h (150 mph)

PIAGGIO MP3

Engine
124 cc/244 cc, liquid-cooled, single-cylinder, four-stroke
Power
124 cc, 11 kW (15 bhp) @ 9250 rpm; 244 cc, 17 kW (23 bhp) @ 8250 rpm
Torque
124 cc, 12 Nm (9 ft lb) @ 8500 rpm; 244 cc, 21 Nm (15 ft lb) @ 6750 rpm
Gearbox
Automatic
Final drive
Direct
Weight
124 cc, 199 kg (439 lb); 244 cc, 204 kg (450 lb)
Top speed
124 cc, 103 km/h (60 mph); 244 cc, 125 km/h (75 mph)

When is a motorcycle not a motorcycle? Probably when it's got three wheels, like the MP3, an entry-level machine designed to instil confidence in new riders by promising not to fall over. In the United Kingdom the MP3 qualifies for the same benefits as a conventional powered two-wheeler, such as congestion-charge exemption and free parking, because the track between its two front wheels is so narrow, and yet the third wheel is sufficient to make this scooter a lot more stable than an ordinary one. The machine leans in exactly the same way as a normal bike and indeed can fall over when stationary, but a thumb-activated locking mechanism is fitted to prevent this happening.

The MP3's innovative parallelogram suspension incorporates a tilt mechanism made from four cast-aluminium control arms with four hinges fixed to the central tube and two guide tubes on either side that are connected to the arms via suspension pins and ball bearings. An electric switch on the handlebars ensures that the tilt mechanism operates only at speeds below 23 km/h (14 mph), while at speeds higher than this the machine handles conventionally.

As well as enabling the MP3 to achieve far greater lean angles than a normal scooter, the three-wheel set-up also reduces braking distances by up to 20 per cent, as a result of the extra tyre area that is in contact with the ground. With its 30-cm (12-in.) diameter wheels and generous proportions, the machine is of similar size to a normal maxi scooter (although perhaps slightly heavier) and is therefore still a practical proposition for nipping through city traffic.

Parking is a cinch, too, as the bike doesn't need to be supported by a centre stand and, because of the tilting mechanism, it can safely be left on quite steep gradients without danger of falling over.

From the front the MP3 looks almost as much like a car as a motorcycle, with its twin headlamps and a nose-mounted radiator grille that is integrated with shock-resistant splash guards that protect the rider from the elements. The rear loading section has been designed to offer maximum passenger comfort and storage capacity. A car-like boot lid (with remote opening) gives access to 65 litres (2.3 cu. ft) of underseat storage for items up to a metre (39.4 in.) long.

Piaggio has already designed a range of dedicated accessories for the MP3, including a 'winter pack' comprising a larger windscreen, hand protectors, thermal tyres, and an electrically heated leg cover. Owners may also specify satellite navigation, a Bluetooth intercom helmet and additional luggage.

SUPERBYKE
ROAD BORE
SUPERBYKE

SUPERBYKE ROAD BORE

The 'mini-moto' craze of a couple of years ago has now turned into a fully fledged nuisance in many countries, with unlicensed, uninsured 'youths' ripping up the streets and parks on cut-price, Asian-built 'not for highway use' machines that, in some cases, are being given away free with mobile-phone subscriptions. In fact, in the UK the mini-moto problem is so bad that legislation aimed at solving it has been tabled in the House of Commons.

One of the suggestions was to ensure that mini-motos are registered like other road vehicles. But this proposal is quite obviously flawed, because the crux of the matter is that these little bikes are so cheap to obtain, whether legally or illegally, and so easily tucked away when not in use, that anyone who chooses to ride one on the road is hardly likely to fit it with a registration plate.

But look at this wacky machine. It's only a tiny bit bigger than a mini-moto, but it is fully road-legal and intended to be ridden by adults rather than children. The strangely named Road Bore offers a surprisingly high specification for its UK price of £995, such as electric and kick-starters, disc brakes front and rear, and a remarkable top speed of 88 km/h (55 mph). Designed for the urban jungle, it will nip through gaps that even a bicycle might struggle to tackle, and parking is a doddle: just pick it up and take it inside. Fuel consumption from the 125-cc, four-stroke engine is pretty amazing, too, at around 64.5 kmpl (180 mpg).

It recalls my first motorcycle, bought for me when I was six: an ex-army Brockhouse Corgi that cost £8 and made me into one of the original mini-moto tearaways.

Engine
125 cc, air-cooled, single-cylinder, four-stroke
Power
6 kW (8 bhp) @ 8000 rpm
Torque
N/A
Gearbox
Five-speed
Final drive
Chain
Weight
70 kg (154 lb)
Top speed
88 km/h (55 mph)

TOMOS RACING 50

Engine
49 cc, single-cylinder, two-stroke
Power
N/A
Torque
N/A
Gearbox
Single-speed automatic
Final drive
Chain
Weight
50 kg (110 lb) (est.)
Top speed
56 km/h (35 mph)

Tomos was founded in the former Yugoslavia in 1956 and became known throughout Eastern Europe as a producer of inexpensive, practical, lightweight motorcycles and 49-cc mopeds. But it was not until the 1980s that the make gained a foothold on the rest of the continent. After a factory opened at Epe in The Netherlands, neighbouring countries became familiar with the Tomos 50 step-through moped, which for some years was about the cheapest road-legal powered two-wheeler on the market. The company now claims to supply 80 per cent of the world's two-wheeled mopeds.

The Tomos reputation for making bargain machines is still intact, although the models in the range are a lot more funky than the pedal-start mopeds of twenty-five years ago, as demonstrated by the Racing 50. Chunky tyres, sturdy, off-road-style handlebars and a high-level exhaust pipe give it a go-anywhere look, and its beady, faired-in headlamps and clear-lens indicators give it a contemporary appearance that will be prized by the teenagers at whom it is aimed.

As an exercise in 'form follows function' design simplicity, the Racing 50 is difficult to beat, with its one-piece frame, compact rear suspension, comfortable saddle and small but useful load platform. Its compact size makes it easy to park, and its lack of superfluous components makes it difficult to damage. Every urban home should have one.

ELECTRIC3W

VECTRIX ELECTRIC 3W

The previous edition of *The New Motorcycle Yearbook* introduced the Vectrix scooter, the first really well-made, practical, high-performance electric two-wheeler to go on general sale. Only now is the machine being taken up in worthwhile numbers, but already Vectrix has unveiled plans to launch a three-wheeled version that will compete with the innovative triple-wheeled offerings from Piaggio and Gilera about which you can also read in this section.

Naturally, the point of the Vectrix's third wheel is to entice newcomers out of their cars and on to a scooter. Being among the first to offer the third-wheel option is an important marketing strategy for the company, as it could win it customers who have never before ridden a petrol-powered two-wheeler and who could, if the Vectrix serves them well, turn into loyal supporters of greener, electrically powered machines.

The only potential shadow over the success of the Electric 3W is its price. Because the electric technology is still fairly new, it is likely to have a higher price tag than, say, the hot-performing Gilera Fuoco. This means that anyone buying the Vectrix will have to be passionate enough about being green not to mind spending quite a bit extra to prove it.

Engine
Brushless-electric, direct-current, radial air-gap motor
Power
20 kW (27 bhp) @ 3000 rpm
Torque
65 Nm (48 ft lb) from standstill
Gearbox
Automatic with slow-speed reverse
Final drive
Direct
Weight
218 kg (480 lb) (est.)
Top speed
100 km/h (62 mph)

KEY DESIGNERS

MIGUEL GALLUZZI

Aprilia

Miguel Galluzzi will go down in history as one of the most important and influential motorcycle designers of the twentieth century. The reason? He created what has become one of the most successful, inspirational and best-loved machines ever to roll off a production line – the iconic Ducati Monster.

It was during the summer of 1990 that Argentinian-born Galluzzi sketched out his first rough drawings for a 'naked' 750-cc motorcycle with a large, round headlamp, bulbous fuel tank and truncated rear end. The frame and engine were left visible and, as with many great designs, the beauty of the creation lay in its simplicity.

And then what happened? Nothing. For more than two years the bike that was later to set the world alight existed only as a paper sketch and a single, embryonic prototype that had been cobbled together from a few left-over components and pushed to one side in the Ducati design studio. It remained that way until Claudio Castiglioni – boss of the Cagiva group, which then owned the brand – showed the 'concept' machine to a select band of importers and their universal approval led to a hasty, completed Monster being made the centrepiece of the Ducati stand at the 1992 Cologne motorcycle show.

It was the birth of a legend, and more than fifteen years later the Monster remains one of the most recognizable and most popular motorcycles on the market, with more than 250,000 examples having taken to the world's streets. This is a machine with universal appeal, for such versions as the restricted-output, 600-cc model attract learner riders as easily as the high-performance S4R model attracts veterans, who love the knockout punch of its 97-kW (130-bhp) engine and the legendary Ducati handling.

Just as significantly, perhaps, the bike helped make motorcycles a cool, luxury accessory, with the Monster virtually becoming the default choice of sports and movie celebrities who wanted to show they were sufficiently down-to-earth to be bikers, too. Its eye-catching looks also made it a popular choice among the makers of advertising campaigns for other products, who frequently chose a Monster as a photo-shoot accessory, affording Ducati additional, and invaluable, worldwide publicity.

Many people regard the arrival of the Monster as the start of the trend of the 'naked' motorcycles that are now an essential part of the production line-up for every major manufacturer. But, far from the formula having been 'done to death', Galluzzi is convinced that naked bikes still have a long way to go and, just a few months into his tenure as head of the Aprilia Style Centre, he is already showing that there is plenty of the old magic left in his pen. Look at the many machines in the Street, Naked and Muscle section of this book (pp. 126–75) – among which you will find the Aprilia Mana and Shiver – and see if you don't agree.

Galluzzi's motorcycling roots go back much further than to the origins of the Ducati Monster, however: his grandfather was a well-known motorcycle racer in Argentina, where he competed during the 1920s in dirt oval races on stripped-down, tuned-up Harley-Davidson

'I have nothing against using the past for inspiration – but only in a way that moves things on'
Miguel Galluzzi

Galluzzi was born with motorcycling in his blood. These images show his grandfather on a Harley-Davidson dirt tracker (left) and his father road racing during the 1950s.

works machines. His high-octane passion was passed down to his sons, Galluzzi's father and uncle, who raced both motorcycles and cars, and Galluzzi himself began riding dirt bikes at the age of eight.

'My love for motorcycles started very young, probably because I grew up among the smell and sound of racing machines, both two-wheeled and four-wheeled – my father even built his own racing car', Galluzzi recalls. 'As I became older it became obvious that I was going to have to try to make my love of bikes and cars part of my working life, and that's when I found out about the Pasadena Art Center College of Design in California. I enrolled and completed the course very quickly, in just three years, because I was so keen to start applying what I was learning.'

That was back in 1986, a time when it was far more sensible, and more popular, to choose a career in automotive rather than in motorcycle design. As a result, Galluzzi took a job with Opel in Germany, where he worked on such 'bread-and-butter' cars as the hatchback Corsa and the Omega saloon before being made senior designer on the Vectra project.

It was at Opel that Galluzzi came into contact with Hideo Kodama, a leading figure with Honda Europe, who in 1989 invited him to move to Italy, where the Japanese firm was planning to establish a design studio.

'Honda sent me to Italy so that I could open a design office in Milan and help create designs that were at the cutting edge of European styling', says Galluzzi.

'But it wasn't long before I moved to the Cagiva group, where I worked on all the different brands, including Morini, Husqvarna, and Ducati. I even designed a scooter as part of a joint venture with a Taiwanese company.'

Although he was to make his name with the Monster, Galluzzi had already penned some significant motorcycles, such as the Ducati 900SS, which was especially interesting at the time because, at the start of the trend for aerodynamic, plastic-clad sports bikes, it made do with a minimalist half fairing.

'Just looking at the beautiful Ducati twin-cylinder engine and the lovely trellis frame made me think that it was wrong to cover it all up, so I proposed the half-fairing design that shows off the engineering as much as possible', explains Galluzzi. 'If it had been up to me, that would have been the only version of the Super Sport that was made, but the commercial department said that if we had a half-fairing version we should offer a full-fairing version too, so I designed a lower section that didn't overwhelm the whole machine.'

At the same time Galluzzi was working on the revival of the Husqvarna brand and designed every motocross, enduro and supermoto bike produced since 1997, as well as the Monster-esque Cagiva Planet and Cagiva Raptor and Xtra Raptor, these last two taking design cues from the wing shapes and beaks of birds of prey.

At the end of 2006, however, Galluzzi was 'poached' by the increasingly aggressive Aprilia brand (owned by the multi-make Piaggio group), which intends to make

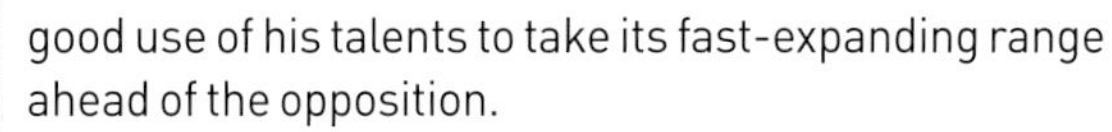

good use of his talents to take its fast-expanding range ahead of the opposition.

'I have been very impressed by the sheer passion that everyone at Aprilia shows for motorcycles,' Galluzzi says, 'and this job really feels as though it will satisfy my need for new goals and new challenges. There is just so much happening, so much to get involved in – from the development of the new four-cylinder engine to an entire range of off-road bikes – and the great thing for me is that Aprilia is very much into naked motorcycles.'

So can we expect a new machine that will create as much of a stir as the Ducati Monster did fifteen years ago?

'Well, that would be nice, wouldn't it?' says Galluzzi. 'There is no doubt that the naked bike scene is still very strong, and I think it will continue to grow. There are many variations on the theme still to be attempted: it is rather like pasta – there is just so much you can do with the same basic ingredient. One area that is really interesting me at the moment is probably the most basic part of a motorcycle there is – the wheels. I recently attended a custom show in Padua and saw a few bikes with 23-in. [58.4-cm] diameter wheels, far bigger than usual. That really set my mind racing.'

So it looks as though the next edition of *The New Motorcycle Yearbook* might have some radically wheeled Aprilias in its pages, but what I really want to know is, which machine does the designer of one of the world's best-loved motorcycles keep in his garage, and what – if not the Monster – is his favourite motorcycle of all time?

'Well, I do, of course, have a Ducati Monster for posterity. It is a very special one with an elliptical tube frame. I also have a 1973 Honda Elsinore motocross bike and my favourite motorcycle of all time is the Vincent Black Shadow – but don't expect to see an Aprilia based on that design. I'm not into "retro" creations at all', says Galluzzi. 'I have nothing against using the past for inspiration – but only in a way that moves things on.'

Above, left
Galluzzi's ancestors pose on race bikes.
Above
Galluzzi designed every one of Husqvarna's off-road motorcycles produced between 1997 and 2006.
Opposite
The Cagiva Raptor (top) and the Ducati Monster that came before it share common genes.

CAGIVA

DUCATI
DUCATI
brembo

WILLIAM G. DAVIDSON

Harley-Davidson

When William A. Davidson helped found the Harley-Davidson marque way back in 1903, little could he have known that the motorcycles that he and his partners were creating represented the germ of a legend; or that, more than a century later, Harley-Davidsons would be more popular than ever and his very own grandson would be designing them.

Well, Harley-Davidson certainly became a runaway success, despite a few setbacks along the way, and it is now one of the world's most recognized brands. And William A.'s grandson, William G. Davidson, is regarded as a key figure in the company's design department and something of a legend in the motorcycle world.

'Willie G.', as he is affectionately known, grew up around motorcycles and recalls riding in his father's sidecar as a child. A naturally gifted artist, he graduated from the University of Wisconsin with a degree in graphic art before being accepted at the celebrated Art Center College of Design in Pasadena, California, which has produced so many of the world's great automotive and motorcycle designers.

The fact that Willie G. was immersed in Californian culture at a time when custom-bike building was entering a phase of exceptional creativity led to his being heavily influenced by the 'choppers' and 'bobbers' that backyard builders had created from the large numbers of ex-War Department Harley-Davidsons sold off in the late 1940s.

Once qualified, Willie G. began his career in the design departments of various major car companies, but away from work the old family genes spurred him to turn his hand to building custom motorcycles, and in 1963 he joined Harley-Davidson, where he shook up the old-school management with his radical thoughts about the way Harleys of the future should look.

Willie G.'s idea to create 'factory custom' bikes inspired by the home-grown machines he had encountered in California initially met with a lukewarm reception from the company's more traditional thinkers, but persistence paid off, and eventually one of Willie G.'s designs was allowed to progress from the drawing board to the blacktop. It was the FX 1200 Super Glide, a machine now regarded as a quintessential Harley product and arguably the first true 'cruiser' bike. The Super Glide proved an instant hit, and the model, available in several forms, remains a linchpin of the current H-D line-up.

Having been promoted to Vice President of Styling in 1969 (a position he still holds today), Willie G. was to have an even more significant effect on the future of the firm co-founded by his grandfather when, in the early 1980s, he became one of thirteen of the company's executives who raised sufficient cash to buy back Harley-Davidson from the giant American Machine and Foundry (AMF) organization, which had taken control of it in 1968.

AMF had injected plenty of cash into the business but managed it badly, allowing market share to fall and losses to rise. Dismayed at what was happening to an American icon, Willie G. and his colleagues moved in and set about the arduous task of reinvigorating the

'Part of the Harley imagery has always been that strong v-twin – I've always thought of the engines as jewellery'
Willie G. Davidson

The FX 1200 Super Glide of 1971 was Willie G.'s first important design. A modernized version remains an important part of the line-up today.

brand and returning it to profit. They were successful beyond their wildest dreams, and by the early 1990s Harley-Davidson was well on its way to becoming one of the most successful automotive companies in the world, an achievement attributable to the introduction of the more modern and reliable 'Evolution' v-twin engine and, of course, to the attractive designs that Willie G. and his team had created.

As a result, the bespectacled, beret-wearing Willie G. was inducted into the Motorcycle Hall of Fame in 1999 and, three years later, was made an honorary member of America's Motorcycle Design Association (AMDA). Yet despite his legendary status in the world of motorcycling, and the world of Harley-Davidson in particular, Willie G. has never been interested in distancing himself from biking's grass roots and is just as likely to be found mingling with a group of regular HOG (Harley Owner's Group) fans as he is to be found making a top-level decision at the boardroom table in Milwaukee.

The timing of the AMDA honour could not have been more appropriate, as it occurred just a few months after the unveiling of a machine that is not only one of the most important in the history of Harley-Davidson, but also the one that perhaps reflects Willie G.'s radical thinking better than any other Harley that has gone before. This is project code P4, more widely known as the V-Rod.

An extraordinary departure for Harley-Davidson, the V-Rod was conceived in the mid-1990s, when the firm's management decided that it needed to answer demands from enthusiasts for a bike with traditional Harley style but with levels of power and performance that the marque had never before offered.

The project was kept 'top secret' for the entire six years it took to complete, with the design team banned from discussing it with even their family or closest friends. The basis of the new bike was to be the VR1000 superbike engine, a fire-breathing powerplant used in the marque's racing machines. Apart from its high power output – in road-going production form it would yield 86 kW (115 bhp), around twice that of the average Harley-Davidson – the unit was a significant departure from the norm in being the first water-cooled engine to be fitted in a road-going Harley.

To some extent, the engine was the easy part; the difficult bit was creating a motorcycle of such high performance that could also be instantly recognized as being a Harley-Davidson. And that responsibility, of course, fell to Willie G. and his design team.

'We don't often have the opportunity of concepting an entire motorcycle from the ground up', Willie G. says. 'I wanted this vehicle to have the type of presence where people would walk up and say, "Wow – that's a Harley-Davidson!" We decided to give it a minimal, aggressive look drawn from drag racing and for the frame to be simple, direct and something that could almost be hung on the wall as a work of art as well as being a place to put an engine. Part of the Harley imagery has always been that strong v-twin – I've always thought of the engines as jewellery, and to maintain the look we added

air fins to the V-Rod's engine, although it is water-cooled and doesn't really need them. It was simply a stylistic touch.

'And that radiator caused a problem, too, because we've never had a big piece of "real estate" hanging on our down tubes. The first one we tried was tiny, but it didn't work, so we had to return to the drawing board.'

The first running prototype was completed in 1998, and Willie G. was the first person to ride it – and promptly broke the gearbox! 'I laugh now, but maybe it was not so funny on the day', he recalls. 'I managed to lock it in fourth gear, but I had still got to ride it and it made me smile from ear to ear. I knew what we were making was something totally different, but it was definitely a true Harley-Davidson.'

With the basic engineering principles in place, it was a matter of refining the machine's overall design and making sure that everything fitted together. Willie G. and his team took advantage of the double-down-tube frame and underseat fuel storage by creating a small, dragster-style gas tank that nestled between the top frame rails; the steering head and frame geometry were calculated to create a raked-out look while ensuring that the V-Rod still had the sharpest handling in the sports-cruiser market; and for the overall finish a unique, brushed-aluminium look was chosen.

The result dropped plenty of jaws when the covers were pulled off at the 2002 Harley-Davidson dealer meeting in Los Angeles, and the V-Rod has gone on to achieve worldwide sales success, both in its original guise and in the several modified versions that have since been included in the line-up – the latest of which is the Night Rod Special (see pp. 74–75).

And, were they around today, those 1960s Harley-Davidson board members who were so reluctant to let Willie G.'s imagination run free would have no option but to admit that he was right all along. After all, as one Harley-Davidson employee recently put it: 'The Willie G. touch – it's something magic.'

Above
Willie G.'s influence has extended from such highway cruisers as the Sportster 1200 (left) to all-out racing machines, including this fire-breathing VR1000 of 1994 (right).

Opposite
Perhaps the designer's most radical project was the styling of the V-Rod, which combines the instantly recognizable Harley-Davidson look with exceptional performance.

ARNOLD WAGNER
PERAVES

More than thirty years ago two British motorcycle enthusiasts set about designing a radical machine that would be ridden in the 'feet-forward' position, powered by an 850-cc Reliant car engine and, most unusually, be covered by a full-length canopy to protect the rider from the elements.

Called the Quasar, this vehicle combining the thrills and handling of a motorcycle with the weather-beating benefits of a small car, might have been a runaway success had it been launched in another era. During the mid-1970s, however, motorcycle sales were close to being at an all-time low, and there was virtually no appetite among buyers for a fresh approach to powered two-wheeled transport.

As a result, a mere twenty-two Quasars were built, but among aficionados of feet-forward motorcycling – and there are more of them about than you might imagine – this strange, almost space-age machine is still regarded as a brave attempt at taking motorcycling into the future. This was hardly an unrealistic vision, because in the 1990s BMW revisited Quasar thinking with its moderately successful C1 scooter, which was designed to entice drivers from four wheels to two with the promise of decent weather protection by similar, canopy-style bodywork.

Yet the Quasar was far from being the first two-wheeler to have car-like pretensions. As long ago as the 1920s a US-based designer named Carl Neracher produced the Ner-a-Car, a motorcycle with a laid-back, feet-forward riding position, of which more than 6000 were built under licence in the United Kingdom before the company that produced them folded in about 1928.

The first fully enclosed motorcycle, however, was the Mauser Einspur Auto, which was built in Germany during the Second World War, and it was this machine that led, if indirectly, to the development of the newly launched Monotracer (see pp. 228–29). The reason for this is that a Czech designer named Jan Anderele was so intrigued by the idea of a covered two-wheeler that, after moving to Western Europe at the height of Communist rule, he began to develop a prototype 'cabin' motorcycle. It caught the attention of a Swiss commercial airline pilot (and champion aerobatic flyer), Arnold Wagner, who thought the basic concept could be developed and taken into the twenty-first century.

Wagner's son, Felix, takes up the story: 'My father believed there was a market for a motorcycle that had all the advantages of a car but the driving fun and leaning abilities of a motorcycle, so in the early 1980s he created a prototype machine called an Ecomobile that was powered by a BMW flat-twin engine and had fully enclosed bodywork.

'It was so well received that he adapted the design to use the BMW K1200 four-cylinder engine and had the first Ecomobile homologated in 1987. Since then ninety have been sold, mainly to enthusiasts in central Europe but some to the UK and America, too.'

Production of the Ecomobile came to an abrupt halt in 2006, when the wooden factory and all the bodywork moulds were destroyed by fire, but the Wagners quickly

'There was a market for a motorcycle that had all the advantages of a car but the driving fun and leaning abilities of a motorcycle'
Arnold Wagner

Monotracers lend a space-age feel to a Swiss village.

conjured up a phoenix from the ashes by launching the Monotracer, a unique machine with enclosed, torpedo-like bodywork and, most unusually, four wheels. Their firm, Peraves, is based in Winterthur, near Zurich, and production of the beautifully engineered and expensively built machines is completed in the Czech Republic.

'The bodywork is highly aerodynamic and very similar to a glider's fuselage', explains Felix, who now runs the company with his brother, Urs. 'It is a two-seater machine with a luggage capacity of 250 litres [8.8 cu. ft] and a top speed of 250 km/h [155 mph]. The rider wears a seatbelt, but no crash helmet as the bodywork provides crash protection – the intention was to create the perfect combination of sports-car handling with the high power-to-weight ratio and convenience of a motorcycle.'

What is probably the most unusual aspect of the Monotracer, however, is that it is a motorcycle that has four wheels rather than two – although it is most definitely not a car.

'Anyone who can ride a conventional motorcycle should be able to ride a Monotracer quite easily, but there is one major difference and that, of course, is the fact that it has a stabilizing wheel on either side of the bodywork', says Felix. 'This takes a little bit of getting used to, because at anything above 3–5 km/h (2–3 mph) the side wheels are kept in the retracted position, but, when the rider wants to stop, the wheels must be deployed. Learning how to do it smoothly and at the correct time is a little like learning to change gear in a car without making a crunch.'

The fact that getting to grips with a Monotracer is not just a simple matter of riding it exactly like you would a motorcycle means that anyone who buys one has to undergo a training course with the Wagners before he or she can ride off into the sunset on their new machine. For a start, the clutch is operated by a foot pedal, the gears are changed by electric switch on the left handlebar, and, most alien of all, the retractable side wheels are activated by a thumb switch that instantly lowers or raises them.

Monotracer novices learn to ride the machine with the wheels in the down position so that they act rather like stabilizers on a child's bicycle (a configuration that is also useful for riding in snow and ice). Once this has been mastered it is time to graduate to 'undercarriage retracted' mode – at which point most people drop the machine on to its pod-like side. But the clever design means that no damage is done because the machine comes to rest on one or other of the side wheels, if at a rather alarming angle.

'Once a rider has got used to the differences it is a very rewarding machine', says Felix. 'The handling is excellent, and when you really get up speed through a series of bends it is possible to touch the side wheels down on the road, such are the potential lean angles – and, because of its long wheelbase, the Monotracer actually becomes more stable the faster it is travelling. Its aerodynamic shape also makes it very economical –

it is easy to achieve an average fuel consumption of around 22 kmpl (60 mpg).'

The Monotracer is powered by the latest version of BMW's K-Series four-cylinder, fuel-injected motorcycle engine – from the RS sports tourer – which is mated to a modified gearbox that has a reverse in order to make this undeniably heavy (460-kg/1014-lb) machine a bit less hard to manoeuvre in and out of tight spaces. The design also allows removal of the gearbox from the Monotracer with the engine *in situ*, and such service items as brake pads require little more effort to replace than they do on a conventional BMW bike, although any major work is unlikely to be easily tackled by the amateur mechanic.

So the theory is a good one, and the practice appears to be everything anyone could have hoped for, and more, but the question is, will it catch on? In a bid to increase sales figures sharply over those achieved for the Ecomobile, the price of the Monotracer has been dramatically reduced to a little over 50,000 euros, compared with around 75,000 euros for its predecessor.

Even at 50,000 euros, however, the Monotracer is still in a price bracket occupied by only the most exotic of limited-production superbikes and, with those protruding side wheels, it is probably not the ideal machine for cutting through city traffic during rush hour – even if it is just about narrow enough to justify some nifty, motorcycle-style overtaking moves to beat the jams.

The Monotracer's selling points, therefore, are its novelty value, its weather-beating practicality, its suitability for prolonged, high-speed cruising without causing the fatigue normally associated with a conventional motorcycle and, of course, the huge fun factor. It is the last of these, I suspect, that will lead most wealthy petrolheads to purchase one of these machines – not the fact that they are hoping to save the planet by downshifting from a four-wheeled car.

Above, left
Arnold Wagner, founder of the company, settles into the cockpit of a Monotracer.
Top
Urs Wagner with a version of the Turbo Mono, a predecessor of the current Monotracer.
Above
View from the cockpit of a 1988 Ecomobile.

Above
Monotracers are entirely hand-built to exacting standards.

Left and below
Some of Wagner's original design drawings for the Ecomobile, pictured below on the test track.

Below, left
British Peraves enthusiast Paul Blezard stands between the two-seater Ecomobile (left) and the more sporting Turbo Mono. In 1988 Blezard was the first person in Britain to receive the JAV Ecomobile Pilot's Licence.

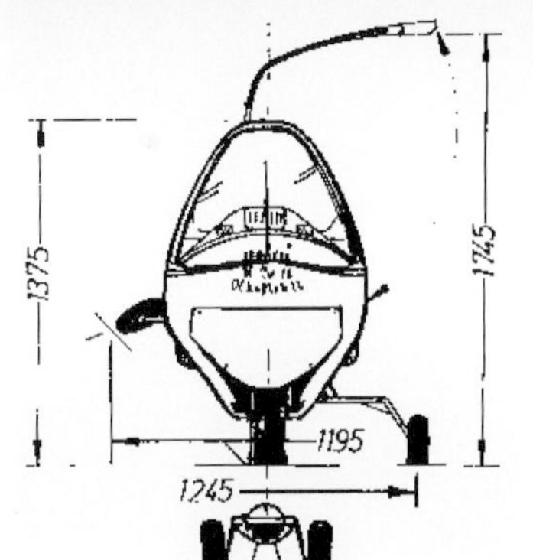

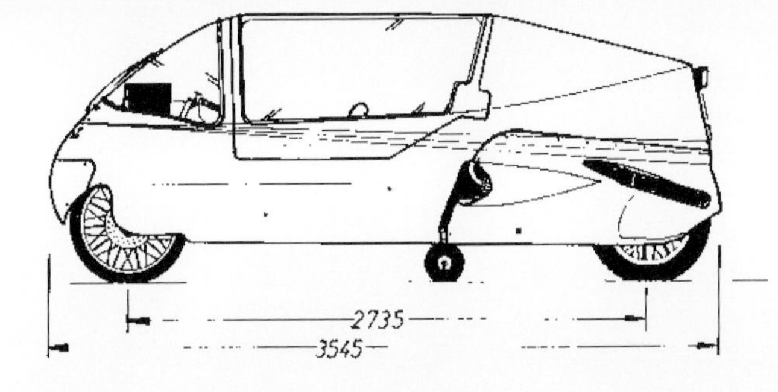

PERAVES AG Winterthur (Schweiz)
W-18 OEkoMobil Wa 24982

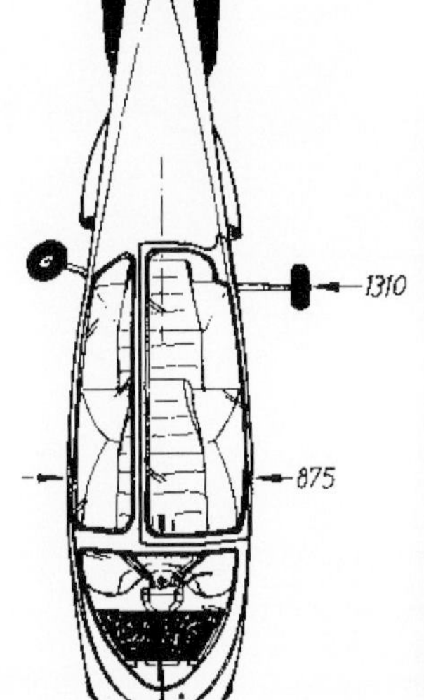

GSX
SUZUKI
GSX
SUZUKI

MOTORCYCLE TYPES

SPORTS

The ability of motorcycle manufacturers to transfer one year's racetrack experience to the next year's model range is extraordinary. Two-wheeled race technology reaches the road far more quickly than comparable advances in the car world, so much so that most road-going machines have the brakes, power and handling to make them competitive racers straight from the crate.

Huge leaps in engineering mean that 600-cc engines are now producing more power than the one-litre units of the 1980s, and extensive use of aluminium, magnesium, titanium and carbon fibre results in chassis that are light and rigid.

Combined with twenty-first-century suspension and tyre and braking technology, this makes for superb-handling machines that are blindingly fast. At the same time, clever electronic mapping of fuel and ignition systems ensures that a motorcycle capable of 290 km/h (180 mph) can still be relied on to behave itself in city traffic.

As for comfort, you can forget it. Sports bikes are uncompromising, racetrack refugees that demand a jockey crouch from the rider and come into their own on a ribbon of twisting blacktop where pillion passengers just don't belong.

SUPERMOTO

Whoever thought of combining a motocross track with short stretches of metalled race circuit created an entirely new category of motorcycle that has taken the two-wheeled world by storm.

Supermotos are what you get when you put a set of wide wheels with sticky road tyres on to an off-road motorcycle. The latest models shamelessly bring out the hooligan in every rider. Firm, long-travel suspension, wasp-slim dimensions, monster disc brakes and, most importantly, a big-bore, four-stroke, single-cylinder engine put the fun back into motorcycling.

Many buyers are converted former sports-bike riders who find a supermoto can fulfil their need for thrills with its lightning handling, punchy, wheelie-prone engine and the type of stopping power that will easily stand the machine on its nose. Most of these bikes have a top speed of around 129 km/h (80 mph), which makes it harder for over-eager riders to lose their licences, and, as well as making great commuter machines, they offer an inexpensive way into competition, for supermoto racing provides thrill-a-minute fun on tight, twisty kart tracks.

TRAIL

A trail (not trails, trial or trials) bike is a road-going motorcycle with off-road capability. It has a softly tuned engine, compliant, long-travel suspension, decent ground clearance and, usually, room for a passenger. A trail bike, therefore, is not an all-out off-road racing machine, but a machine that is just as at home on a green lane in the country as it is being used for commuting in the city.

The most popular trail bikes used to have an engine capacity of 250 cc or less. Usually two-strokes, they were light, nimble and easy to drag out of a muddy ditch. Now stricter emission rules and the mass use of lightweight materials have led to the quieter, cleaner four-stroke engine being more favoured. A 250-cc, four-stroke trail bike is now lighter, niftier and more forgiving than the two-strokes of old, and most are equipped with suspension systems that, not so long ago, would have been found only on state-of-the-art motocross racers.

ENDURO

Enduro motorcycles are similar to trail bikes, only more competition-orientated and sometimes nothing more than road-legal motocrossers. An enduro is a type of off-road trial in which competitors are required to cover large distances over difficult terrain against the clock.

CRUISER

Harley-Davidson started it all with its large-capacity, laid-back, v-twin groundshakers that remain the stuff of dreams and legend. The company is the world's most successful producer of cruiser bikes, but competition continues to hot up in a category of machine that many riders believe epitomizes the freedom of motorcycling.

A cruiser doesn't need to be fast; it just needs to have presence. The v-twin engine has emerged as the classic powerplant, and the larger the capacity the better. Make the frame long and low, make the handlebars wide and high, and put the footrests well forward. Pad the saddle and add lashings of chrome, a fat back tyre and exhausts as mean-sounding as the law will allow. Then you've got a cruiser.

Buyers are often 'born-again' bikers with cash to spend, who like the low seat height and loping gait that cruisers offer. The latest bikes handle surprisingly well, too, and with a range of models from every maker, a cruiser no longer has to be a Harley – although for purists, it does really.

ADVENTURE SPORTS

When such manufacturers as BMW, Yamaha and Honda introduced their first big four-stroke trail machines in the early 1980s, riders discovered a whole new world of motorcycling. They found that these large, comfortable machines were ideal for exploring difficult-to-reach parts of the world. The motorcycles' off-road credentials meant they could ford rivers and cross deserts; their lazy engines provided an adequate cruising speed; and their imposing size gave them the luggage-carrying ability of a small camel.

Spring-loaded gear and brake levers, flexible indicator stems and lightweight, plastic mudguards protected the machines from the knocks and bumps of unmetalled roads, and large-capacity fuel tanks lessened the problem of the lack of filling stations in remote areas.

These motorcycles heralded today's adventure-sports machines, more of which are now sold than any other category of motorcycle. The latest have powerful, twin-cylinder engines, bikini fairings blended into their fuel tanks, and unfeasibly sharp handling. With numerous after-market accessories available to enhance their considerable capability for adventure, they have truly made the world a smaller place.

TOURER

Thirty years ago the hardened long-distance rider had little choice of motorcycle. BMW's shaft-drive, flat-twins had carved out a niche as definitive touring machines, and Honda was starting to offer competition, with its luxurious, water-cooled Gold Wing. These apart, it was a matter of throwing a set of panniers over your faithful all-rounder and heading for the hills.

Today it is a very different story, with every serious manufacturer offering superbly equipped, large-engined, purpose-built touring bikes that are as well appointed as some family cars.

Aerodynamically efficient fairings protect rider and passenger from the elements at three-figure cruising speeds, ergonomically designed seats ensure day-long comfort, and intercom-linked sound systems relieve motorway monotony. Handlebar grips (and seats) are invariably heated, fuel tanks can offer a range of more than 402 km (250 miles), and modular luggage systems that lock on to purpose-built carrying racks provide capacious, stylish, and secure storage.

SPORTS TOURER

What we call a 'sports tourer' nowadays would, not so long ago, have been regarded as a hyper-sports race replica. The power and handling of these machines leave old-school sports bikes for dead, yet they also manage to be surprisingly practical.

With less radical riding positions than their more uncompromising pure sports cousins, sports tourers accommodate rider and passenger in reasonable comfort over long distances. A wealth of luggage has been designed to fit around their curvaceous flanks and tanks, yet the sleek appearance of the average sports bike won't leave would-be racers feeling embarrassed that they are not riding the real thing.

In fact, for those willing to admit that all-out sports bikes are too uncomfortable and needlessly fast for daily use, such sports tourers as Honda's VFR 800 and Triumph's Sprint ST have come to be regarded as true all-rounders.

STREET

Street bikes are best described as 'traditional' motorcycles: not glamorous, not especially sporty, not madly fast and not always state-of-the-art. These are machines based on tried-and-tested engineering, sometimes slightly old-fashioned looks and the simple principle of motorcycle as workhorse. Engines range in size from 250 cc to 750 cc, and the bikes sell to commuter riders who appreciate their reliability and lack of pretension.

NAKED

No sooner had the first sports bikes emerged during the early 1980s than riders were ripping off the fairings, junking the dropped handlebars in favour of upright ones, and creating mean-looking 'streetfighter'-style custom bikes that exposed once more the artwork of engineering.

Twenty years later and the major manufacturers are making streetfighters, now commonly called 'naked' bikes, the likes of which the DIY customizers of the 1980s could only have dreamed of.

Usually derived from pure sports models, naked bikes offer an upright riding position that makes them more practical for everyday riding, yet their engines are only mildly detuned and, with their state-of-the-art sports suspension, they handle equally well. Aggressive twin exhausts tucked beneath seats, fat tyres and unconventionally shaped headlamps are currently *de rigueur* on nakeds.

It is hard to believe that the mean looks of the latest nakeds could ever be improved upon, but in reality, of course, they surely will be.

MUSCLE

Muscle bikes follow the same basic principles as street bikes but derive their description from the large-capacity, multi-cylinder engines that power them. Consequently, they are big machines with significant presence, and they require a fair amount of muscle to handle.

Such models as Suzuki's Bandit 1200, Yamaha's XJR1300 and Kawasaki's ZRX1200 have been around for years now, but they continue to have a strong following among riders who like a motorcycle to look like a motorcycle and who appreciate the bullet-proof engines and comfortable, upright riding positions that muscle bikes offer.

RETRO

There are plenty of older motorcyclists who regard some of the British and Italian machines of the 1970s through rose-tinted goggles; but the fact is, although they looked like rolling works of art, many of these bikes were less than reliable.

Motorcycle technology has come on by leaps and bounds since then. The electrics are better; engines are more powerful, more efficient and more reliable; and the materials and methods used in frame-building make modern chassis that are lighter, stronger and more rigid.

Imagine if those great-looking old bikes had been this good. Well, it seems, they can be now. Such firms as Triumph and Ducati have produced modern-day versions of the 1970s classics and have managed to bring the style we love right up to date in a modern package. Royal Enfield is back, too, with a modernized version of the Bullet, equipped with electric start and five gears.

SCOOTER

The word 'scooter' used to refer only to the instantly recognizable Vespas, Lambrettas and the like, which have become as much a part of Italian culture as pizza and ice cream, but modern scooters come in all shapes and sizes and from manufacturers all over the world. An unwritten rule seems to dictate that once a scooter's engine exceeds 250 cc it becomes a 'maxi' or 'super' scooter, but otherwise anything goes. The main features of a scooter are that it has a platform and leg shields rather than exposed footrests, its engine is enclosed, and invariably it has 'twist-and-go' transmission, which makes it easy and convenient to ride. Underseat storage space is also desirable and, whereas small wheels were once universal, many scooter riders prefer the added stability provided by the larger rims often found on the latest models.

Three-figure maximum speeds, single-figure 0–97-km/h (0–60 mph) times and relaxed long-distance cruising ability were at one time never associated with scooters, because they had small engines and tiny wheels and worked best in strictly urban environments.

MAXI SCOOTER

The emergence of the first maxi scooters in the late 1990s changed attitudes to their predecessors. They took the automatic, twist-and-go ease of scooter riding to a new level, with their half-litre engines, aerodynamic fairings and bigger wheels. Maxi scooters can carry two in comfort and mix it in the motorway fast lane with confidence; they're even good for touring.

Practicality, however, is the crux of the maxi scooter. These machines offer a useful amount of storage space, their protective bodywork means you need not turn up at the office looking dishevelled, and the most sophisticated models boast such features as heated handlebars, stereo systems, electrically adjustable screens and mobile-telephone chargers.

ODDBALL

As components become cheaper and easier to produce, consumers demand new forms of entertainment, and as conventions become ever more irrelevant, motorcycle designers become all the more imaginative.

So it's no surprise that a new, unclassifiable form of powered two-wheeler is emerging that has been strongly influenced by skateboard and BMX culture. These bikes take knocks and bumps in their stride, ooze street cred and, in some cases, can be used to perform far-out stunts.

Included in the Oddball section of this book you will find everything from a high-performance electric scooter to a stunt bike that is so pared down it is almost more bicycle than motorbike. There is even one machine powered by a helicopter engine and a Harley-Davidson dragster that can be bought off the shelf and ready to race.

GLOSSARY

Italics indicate a cross-reference.

AIR COOLING
Air-cooled engines rely on the passage of air to dissipate heat from around the engine and, usually, are heavily finned for this purpose.

AIR FILTER
A foam or corrugated-card device that prevents airborne foreign matter, such as dust and water, from entering the fuel-delivery system.

AIRBOX
A chamber attached to a *carburettor* or fuel-injection system through which air is supplied to enable vaporization of fuel to take place. Also acts as a housing for the *air filter.*

ANTI-LOCK BRAKING SYSTEM (ABS)
A system to prevent loss of control caused by a wheel locking on slippery surfaces or under extreme braking. ABS electronically releases and restores braking pressure at intervals of fractions of a second to prevent wheel locking.

BASH PLATE
Protective metal guard often used on off-road or dual-purpose machines to prevent damage to the underside of the motorcycle engine by stones and other debris.

BELT DRIVE
A clean and quiet method of transferring power from the gearbox to the driven wheel via a flexible toothed belt, as opposed to a chain or driveshaft. Particularly favoured by Harley-Davidson.

BHP (BRAKE HORSEPOWER)
The imperial unit of measurement of the power developed by an engine. The corresponding metric unit is the kilowatt (kW) (1 bhp = 0.7457 kW).

BORE
The diameter of an individual *cylinder* in an engine, inside which the piston travels.

CALIPER
The part of a *disc brake* that presses brake pads on to the brake disc to slow the wheel.

CAMSHAFT
The part of an engine that controls the opening and closing of the inlet and exhaust valves that draw in vaporized fuel and expel spent gases. Many motorcycles have *double overhead camshafts*.

CAPACITY
A measure of engine size, referred to as 'cc' (cubic centimetres). A 1-litre engine is described as '1000 cc'. In the United States engine capacity is measured in cubic inches (1 cubic in. = 16.4 cc).

CARBON FIBRE
A very light and strong material made of woven and bonded carbon that is often used to produce ancillary parts for high-performance motorcycles.

CARBURETTOR
A device that mixes fuel and air in the correct quantities and feeds it into an engine to enable internal combustion.

CASSETTE GEARBOX
A modular gear cluster that can quickly be removed from a motorcycle engine and replaced with an alternative set of gears to give different ratios. Most useful on race machines.

CAST-ALLOY WHEEL
A popular type of motorcycle wheel that is light, strong and easy to clean, and can be produced in many styles.

CLUTCH
A component that converts the power of an engine into drive to the *transmission*. The 'slipper' clutch, currently popular on sports bikes, eliminates the danger of the rear wheel locking during downward gear changes at high engine revs.

COMPRESSION RATIO
The ratio of maximum *cylinder* to combustion-chamber volume, when the piston is at the top of its stroke, compared with when it is at the bottom of its stroke.

CON(NECTING) ROD
A part of an engine connecting the rotating *crankshaft* to the piston in order to convert rotation into vertical or horizontal movement.

CRANKCASE
A casing containing the *crankshaft* and gearbox.

CRANKSHAFT
A rotating shaft to which the *connecting rod*(s) is attached.

CYLINDER
A cylindrical chamber in which a piston travels.

CYLINDER HEAD
The 'head' of an engine, containing inlet and exhaust valves and, in an overhead-camshaft engine, the *camshaft*.

DESMODROMIC
A system of valve control used by Ducati, in which a cam, not a spring, opens and closes the engine's valves.

DISC BRAKE
A brake that operates by pressing pads of friction material on to a disc attached to the wheel.

DOUBLE OVERHEAD CAMSHAFT
Usually found in high-performance engines. Two *camshafts* enable the inlet and exhaust valves to be closed and opened more efficiently.

DRUM BRAKE
A brake that operates pressing 'shoes' of friction material on to a cylindrical wall inside a wheel hub.

DRY SUMP
A lubrication system that stores oil in a separate tank, rather than in a sump at the bottom of the engine. Common in racing motorcycles, it prevents a surge of oil during hard braking, accelerating and cornering.

DRY WEIGHT
The weight of a motorcycle without fuel, oil or coolant.

DYNAMOMETER
A machine used to measure engine *torque*, enabling brake horsepower to be calculated.

ELECTRONIC FUEL INJECTION (EFI)
A more efficient but more complicated method of supplying vaporized fuel to the combustion chamber than a *carburettor*.

ENDURO
A type of off-road competition in which riders follow an unseen course in a specified time.

ENGINE BRAKING
The braking effect of an engine when the *throttle* is closed; this is particularly strong on large-capacity, *v-twin* engines.

FENDER
American term for a mudguard.

FLAT TRACKER
A type of motorcycle designed for the oval or 'flat-track' racing that became popular in the United States in the 1930s and remains so today.

FLAT-TWIN
An engine configuration in which the two *cylinders* are horizontally opposed to each other. Also known as 'boxer' configuration.

FLICKABILITY
A colloquial term used to describe the ease with which a motorcycle can be made to change direction at speed; best assessed by riding through a series of sweeping bends.

FOUR-STROKE
An engine that requires four piston strokes per power stroke.

GAS FLOWING
The act of modifying the inlet and exhaust ports of a *cylinder head* in order to improve the flow of fuel vapour into the engine and the exit of exhaust gases.

GEARTRAIN
The system of gears, chains and/or shafts that transmits power from the engine's *crankshaft* to the driven wheel.

GP
Abbreviation of Grand Prix.

HORIZONTALLY OPPOSED
An engine configuration in which the *cylinders* are opposed at 180 degrees to one another.

HUB
The central part of a wheel.

HUGGER
A type of close-fitting rear-wheel mudguard.

INJECTOR
A pressurized nozzle through which a fuel-injection system feeds vaporized fuel into the combustion chamber.

INVERTED FORKS
Front suspension system in which the sliders (the thick sections of the forks) are at the top rather than at the bottom. Inverted forks are currently considered state-of-the-art and are found mainly on high-performance motorcycles, although Suzuki has recently used them on one of its cruiser bikes.

KICK-STARTER
An integral, foot-operated crank used to start a motorcycle's engine.

L-TWIN
An engine configuration in which the *cylinders* are arranged in an 'l' shape, i.e. at, or almost at, a right angle to each other. A typical example is the Ducati twin-cylinder engine, in which the angle between the cylinders is too great for the configuration to be described as 'v'.

LEADING LINK
A type of front suspension in which the wheel spindle is mounted ahead of a pivoted link.

LIQUID COOLING
A method of maintaining an even engine temperature by passing water around the engine through a water jacket linked to a radiator that is cooled by the flow of air. Also known as water cooling.

LONG-STROKE
A term used to describe an engine in which the stroke, or the vertical travel of the piston, exceeds the *bore* of the *cylinder*.

MARQUE
An alternative word for 'make', e.g. BMW, Ducati and Triumph.

OIL COOLING
A method of cooling an engine whereby lubricating oil passes through a radiator. It is used as an additional means of cooling both *air-* and *liquid-cooled* engines.

OVER-SQUARE
A term used to describe an engine in which the *bore* is greater than the stroke, a feature of most modern, high-revving, multi-cylinder motorcycle engines.

OVERBORED
A term used to describe an engine of which the *capacity* has been increased beyond its original size.

PANNIER
A rear-mounted luggage item that is made either of a hard material, such as glass fibre, or of a soft, water-resistant material.

PEAKY
A term used to describe an engine that has a narrow *power band* at high revs and makes little power at lower revs.

POWER BAND
The point in the rev range at which an engine makes its maximum potential power. This is usually somewhat lower than the maximum safe rev limit.

POWERTRAIN
A term that encompasses the engine, gearbox and final-drive units of a motorcycle.

RADIAL BRAKE CALIPER
A brake *caliper* that is fitted by means of bolts running from back to front, rather than from one side to the other, to produce a more equal spread of pressure on the brake pads.

RAM AIR INTAKE
A scoop built into the fairing that is designed to force air into the machine's fuel system at speed, to improve combustion.

REGENERATIVE BRAKING
A system for transferring the kinetic energy produced under braking to electricity used to recharge the machine's batteries.

REV COUNTER
An instrument that measures the revolutions of an engine, usually in thousands per minute. Also known as a tachometer.

ROADABLE
A word used to describe the abilities of a dual-purpose machine on tarmac. A well-designed adventure sports bike, for example, will be capable of crossing a mountain pass but will also perform well on a motorway, meaning it is still 'roadable'.

ROLL ON
The *capacity* of a motorcycle travelling at low engine revs in a high gear to accelerate rapidly and smoothly in the same gear using the engine's *torque*.

RPM
Abbreviation of revolutions per minute.

SHOCK ABSORBER
A term commonly used to describe a rear suspension unit or units.

SIAMESED
A term used to describe an exhaust system on a motorcycle with two or more *cylinders* in which individual exhaust pipes exiting from the engine merge together, usually ending in a single silencer.

SILENCER
A component of an exhaust system that muffles engine noise.

SLIDER
The moving part of a motorcycle fork.

SPARK PLUG
A component used to carry a spark across two electrodes inside an engine's combustion chamber to cause ignition. Twin-plug engines are currently popular for their greater efficiency and lower emissions.

SPEEDOMETER
An instrument used to measure speed of travel.

SPOKED WHEEL
The traditional type of motorcycle wheel, laced with a network of thin wire spokes. Particularly popular on off-road machines because individual spokes break on impact with hard objects and so provide a degree of shock absorption that protects the rim from deformation. A *cast-alloy wheel* may fracture in this situation.

STEERING DAMPER
A telescopic friction device used to counter steering shake at high speed.

SUBFRAME
A separate, detachable part of a chassis at the rear of the main frame.

SUMP
An oil reservoir sited underneath or inside a *crankcase*.

SWING ARM
A chassis component that holds the rear wheel and pivots vertically to enable the operation of the suspension system.

THROTTLE
A term used to describe the handlebar control that regulates fuel flow to the engine, although more accurately it refers to the variable restriction in a *carburettor* or fuel-injection system.

TORQUE
A measure of the force applied to produce rotational movement, measured in foot pounds (ft lb) or Newton metres (Nm). The majority of the torque figures cited in this book are given in Newton metres (1.356 Nm = 1 ft lb). Engines that produce high torque figures at low revs have the best pulling power for hill climbing and can accelerate more smoothly from lower revs in a high gear than less 'torquey' engines. Single- and twin-*cylinder* engines tend to be 'torquey', whereas multi-cylinder engines tend to be 'revvy'.

TRANSMISSION
A system of gears by which engine power is transformed into drive.

TRIPLE CLAMPS
The brackets that attach a motorcycle's front fork assembly to the frame and handlebars.

UNSPRUNG WEIGHT
The part of an engine that lies beneath – i.e. on the road side – of the suspension, such as parts of the wheels, the brakes and a portion of the suspension itself.

V-FOUR
V-four engines are usually arranged as two banks of *cylinders*, in 'v' formation, placed side by side across the motorcycle frame.

V-TWIN
An engine configuration in which twin *cylinders* form a 'v' shape. A typical example is a Harley-Davidson engine.

VALVE
A part of an engine that allows fuel to enter the combustion chamber and waste gases to exit it. Sophisticated, higher-revving engines have several valves in each *cylinder* (five in some Yamaha engines). A four-cylinder engine with four valves per cylinder is referred to as a sixteen-valve engine.

WATER COOLING
See *liquid cooling*.

MOTORCYCLE SHOWS

8–16 SEPTEMBER 2007
Motus, Fiera del Levante, Bari, Italy

26–28 SEPTEMBER 2007
Interbike, Sands Expo and Convention Center, Las Vegas, USA

29 SEPTEMBER – 7 OCTOBER 2007
Mondial du Deux Roues, Paris Expo Porte de Versailles, France

2–4 NOVEMBER 2007
Sydney Motorcycle Show, Sydney, Australia

6–11 NOVEMBER 2007
EICMA Moto, Fiera Milano Nuovo Polo, Milan, Italy

22 NOVEMBER – 2 DECEMBER 2007
International Motorcycle and Scooter Show, National Exhibition Centre (NEC), Birmingham, UK

30 NOVEMBER – 9 DECEMBER 2007
Essen Motor Show, Messe Essen, Germany

7–9 DECEMBER 2007
Toronto Motorcycle Show, Metro Toronto Convention Centre, Toronto, Canada

7–16 DECEMBER 2007
Bologna Motor Show, Bologna, Italy

4–6 JANUARY 2008
Calgary Motorcycle Show, Stampede Park, Calgary, Canada

11–13 JANUARY 2008
Edmonton Motorcycle Show, Northlands Park, Edmonton, Canada

18–20 JANUARY 2008
Bike Expo, Padova Fiere, Padua, Italy

24–27 JANUARY 2008
Vancouver Motorcycle Show, Tradex Exhibition Centre, Abbotsford, British Columbia, Canada

FEBRUARY 2008
MCN London Motorcycle Show, ExCel, London, UK

8–10 FEBRUARY 2008
Quebec City Motorcycle Show, Centre de Foires de Québec, Quebec, Canada

22–24 FEBRUARY 2008
Montreal Motorcycle Show, Montreal Convention Centre, Montreal, Canada

27 FEBRUARY – 2 MARCH 2008
Motorräder, Exhibition Centre Westfallenhalle, Dortmund, Germany

MARCH 2008
Motoexpo, Feira Internacional de Lisboa, Lisbon, Portugal

MARCH 2008
Dhaka International Motor Show, China Friendship Conference Centre, Dhaka, Bangladesh

MARCH 2008
Irish Motorbike and Scooter Show, Royal Dublin Society, Dublin, Ireland

APRIL 2008
Moto Park, Crocus Expo, Moscow, Russia

APRIL 2008
Motocykel, Bratislava Exhibition Ground, Bratislava, Slovakia

APRIL 2008
Taipei Ampa, Taipei World Trade Center, Taiwan

25–28 APRIL 2008
China International Bicycle and Motor Fair, Shanghai New International Expo Center, Shanghai, China

1–4 MAY 2008
Motoshow, Fira de Barcelona, Barcelona, Spain

Kawasaki

SHOEI

ACKNOWLEDGEMENTS

Many thanks to all at Merrell Publishers for making *The New Motorcycle Yearbook* such a successful series. I am especially grateful to the book's designer, David Hawkins, who always makes it look enticing; to its meticulous copy-editor, Richard Dawes; and to my editor, Helen Miles, who has overseen all three editions so brilliantly. She has now moved on and will be sadly missed. The book is dedicated to my girlfriend, Helen Griffith, and our wonderful son, Cosmo, who was born in January just after the feature essay about Soichiro Honda was completed. Unlike my parents, I hope he *does* like motorcycles!

PICTURE CREDITS

The illustrations in this book have been reproduced with the kind permission of the following manufacturers:

Aprilia SpA
Baotian
Benelli
Big Dog Motorcycles
Bimota SpA
BMW
Buell Motorcycles
Cagiva
Can-Am
CCM
CF Moto
Confederate Motor Company
Crocker
Ducati Motor Holding SpA
Duss
eCycle
Gilera, Piaggio & C. SpA
Harley-Davidson Motor Company
Hartford
Honda Motor Co.
Husqvarna Motorcycles
Hyosung
Kawasaki Motors
KTM-Sportsmotorcycle AG
Mantis
Martin Conquest
Moto Guzzi
Moto Morini
MV Agusta
Nacional Motor, S.A.U. (Derbi)
NCR
Peraves
Peugeot
Royal Enfield
Sachs Fahrzeug- und Motorentechnik GmbH
Shelby
Steffano
Suzuki Motor Corporation
Tomos Racing
Triumph Motorcycles Ltd
Vectrix
Vespa
Victory Motorcycles
Vyrus
Wakan
Yamaha Motor Corporation

Thanks also to journalist and photographer Paul Blezard and the staff of Monkeybike.co.uk